A New Identity
for the Priest

A New Identity
for the Priest

Toward an Ecumenical Ministry

by RICHARD H. GUERRETTE

PAULIST PRESS
Paramus, N.J. / New York

Library of Congress
Catalog Card Number: 72-95651

ISBN 0-8091-1764-9

Published by Paulist Press
Editorial Office: 1865 Broadway, N.Y., N.Y. 10023
Business Office: 400 Sette Drive, Paramus, N.J. 07652

Printed and bound in the
United States of America

CONTENTS

v

To

The Emmanuel Servant Community

whose spiritual house and priestly people:

Raymond, Judith, Deanna, Michael, Lawrence, Christopher, and Cynthia Lamy; Andre, Marian, Pierre, Paul, Kim Mai, Thomas and Martin Giroux; Michael, Frances, Elizabeth, Michael and Brian Keilty; Richard Pieterse; Margaret and Gretta Palmer; John, Catherine, Judith, Margaret, Mary Ellen, Jeanne and Elizabeth Lovrin; Roy Langlais; Karen, Maria, Beth and Grace MacNamara; Georgia and Sylvia Giroux; Dennis, Rita and Brendan Michael O'Sullivan; Jean Bernius; Christopher, Maria, Norman, Katherine, Matthew and Jessica Langlois; Liberta D'Antonio; Marcel Lamy; Donald, Luke, Matthew, Maria and Christina Giroux; Ronald and Corinne Lamy; James and Gail Tirrell . . .

are

signs ". . . of present happenings and

things that are still to come." (Rev. 1:20)

If anyone has ears to hear, let him listen to what the Spirit is saying to the churches: to those who prove victorious I will give the hidden manna and a white stone—a stone with a new name written on it, known only to the man who receives it.

Revelation 2:17

FOREWORD

That there is a theological crisis in the church—Catholic and Protestant—is now obvious. That the suddenness of its onset in the post-Vatican Council Catholic Church has created a special problem for Catholic priests is also apparent. "Openness to the world" after all is two-sided. It makes possible renewed dialogue with the modern spirit and intensifies concern for relating the Christian faith to the acute needs of modern man. That is gain. But it also reduces the traditional sense of mystery, of representing the transcendent, the holy, that was associated with priesthood. We can argue that this sense of mystery was no longer directly related to contemporary life—that it was nostalgic in its ebbing power. That is probably true. But until the dialogue of the faith with contemporary life leads to a new sense of the transcendent, we will necessarily face a sense of deep loss.

Father Guerrette seeks to work through this sense of loss, seeking to uncover paths that carry promise of the rediscovery of the role of priesthood by pointing to the transcendent. He believes that such paths are likely to be found where the discipline of theology takes seriously the discipline of sociology and administrative science. By understanding the relation of the theological crisis in the church to the organizational crisis of the church, we will be in a better position to plan for the future of the church's mission.

His analysis deals directly with the Catholic form of the crisis. It explores the inner church situation in the post-Vatican Council period. Then with the help of the tools of social science he makes some preliminary proposals for the directions which the church should take. There is no way back except the way forward; and that way requires the courage of the explorer.

As a Protestant I discovered that while the analysis of the problem reveals differences in timetable between our previously separated Christian confessions, the differences are fast disappearing. We are being thrown together in a common crisis. Let us hope that we will find each other in the common task of finding the faithful path into God's future.

Colin W. Williams
Dean, Yale Divinity School

PREFACE

Like the priest, a good social researcher is one who *serves* those whom he studies. However precise the quality of his data and however scholarly these have been compiled and collated with theory, his work is really in vain unless it is directed toward the improvement of the more humane living or working conditions of his subjects. All too often social researchers have conducted their work in a most unsocial manner, draining their respondents for data through questionnaires and surveys, formulating conclusions and even predicting outcomes without offering any concrete proposals for effecting social change.

Without prejudice to those who have heretofore engaged themselves in research studies on priests, one sometimes wonders whether their lengthy reports have been undertaken with sufficient circumspection into the identity crisis of their subjects as to render them service. Their data have been precise, their questionnaires and surveys, extensive; but priests remain drained and many disconcerted over the unheeded conclusions and the unfulfilled predictions of their studies. While these researchers are certainly not to blame for the failure of the church to implement their recommendations, their efforts were simply not conducted with a view to resolving the crisis through any concrete, practical proposal for effecting pastoral change. Thus, as scholarly as much of this research has been, it has not served priests very well.

As a parish priest involved in socio-religious research, I have attempted in this work to serve those whom I have studied by suggesting such a proposal as a means to resolving the identity crisis in the priesthood. Utilizing some of the precise data of my research associates on the work experiences and career growth of priests and interrelating this material with some organizational theory and a theology of ministry, I have presented this research as a working base on which an integrative sociological plan for the pastoral reform of the church has been constructed with the specific purpose of laying an ecclesiological foundation on which priestly reidentity can be built. From this ecclesiological base, I have formulated some theological constructs for redefining the role of the priest in a plural world and for rebuilding his career in an ecumenical church as the primary prerequisites for his new identity. With such a concrete plan for effecting pastoral change, the church can begin to implement the suggested recommendations for the reidentity of the priest. Thus, as practical as this research is designed to be, it can serve priests very well.

In a search for priestly reidentity, however, more is needed than sociological models and theological constructs for the organizational church. The rebuilding process must involve the priest himself, projecting him toward new heights that rise above institutional structures and clerical forms. For this reason, I have submitted some projections for the priesthood that focus toward an ecumenical ministry. These projections are intended to open the priest to a path of discovery on which he can develop some incentives for searching beyond what he has known and experienced and where he can subsequently find himself in a common quest for ministerial identity not only with his ordained Protestant and Orthodox colleagues but with every Christian.

So transcending one's accustomed level of ministry involves a certain fear of the unknown and that is risk; but it also involves a certain faith in one's mission and that is grace. Jeremiah taught us this. When this prophet acknowledged the risk of his call to the nations and responded to the grace of its ecumenical mission, he found his identity in the prophetic ministry (1:4-19). When the priest acknowledges the risks of his call to serve a plural world and responds to the grace of its ecumenical mission, he will find his identity in an ecumenical ministry.

In response to the grace of this ecumenical mission, I would like to acknowledge all my relatives, friends and associates who have helped to allay the fears in the risks I have had to assume in my own search for priestly reidentity: my father and mother, who have themselves responded to the grace of change; my sister Nancy and her husband John Bandy, who, with their children Jaa and Joann, are themselves transcending their accustomed level of faith with the courage of a Jonathan Livingston Seagull; John and Catherine Lovrin, whose communion has kept me alive through the costs of discipleship; my faithful friends and associates Fathers James Fanelli of the Hartford Archdiocesan School Office and Pierre Minard, O.S.B., of the Hermitage of La Grand Foret in St. Aulaye, France, whose constant professional and prayerful support has been sustaining; Professor George Lindbeck, Father Henri Nouwen, Dean Colin Williams and Associate Dean Harry Adams of Yale Divinity School, who have been supportive sources of direction and encouragement; Professors Douglas Hall of York University in Toronto and Benjamin Schneider of the University of Maryland, who graciously granted me permission to utilize their research data at the Department of Administrative Sciences of Yale University; Professor John Koval of the Department of Sociology of the University of Notre Dame, Brother Didier Piveteau, Professor of Catechesis and Education at the Institut Catholique de Paris and Father Richard McBrien of the Department of Theology at Boston College, who read parts of the manuscript; Professor Raymond Bradt of the Department of Religious Studies at the University of Virginia, whose perceptive insights helped to open my vision to new horizons; and Victor and Ilke Loefflath Ehly, Thomas and Ruth Hummel, Professor Roland Bainton and all my other colleagues and our alumni of the Ecumenical Continuing Education Center at Yale who have offered much constructive feedback in the development of my theories. I would finally like to thank my brothers and sisters of the Emmanuel Servant Community of the Archdiocese of Hartford and all the priests who have helped them to reidentify in their mission. Their trusted love and devotion have inspired me with burning incentives to record in this book our common experiences toward an ecumenical ministry.

Ecumenical Continuing Education Center at Yale
New Haven, Connecticut

CHAPTER I

IDENTITY CRISIS

OF THE PRIEST

While the church has organized its priesthood into a hierarchical system of clerical ministers for many theological and historical reasons, it has not provided its priests with adequate organizational resources to promote their psychological success and career growth in the ministry. Priests have not ordinarily been assigned to positions where their human rights have been so respected as to allow for their personal development in the priesthood. Neither have they been permitted to function in their positions so as to fulfill their duties through professional collaboration in the ministry. Their personal dignity has been commonly violated by their having been impeded from acting freely and responsibly in their assignments. In such organizational conditions, which have developed from unfavorable authority relationships with their superiors, many priests have lost their ministerial identity.

Since the promulgation of the decrees of the Second Vatican Council which have called for significant changes in the role of the priest in the modern world,[1] scores of priests, anxious to reclaim their dignity and to recapture their identity, are still waiting for the implementation of these changes in the particular situations of their work assignments.

It is the purpose of this book to respond to those who are waiting by providing more abundant pastoral resources through which priests can acquire psychological success to grow in the ministry and to reidentify in the priesthood. This response must begin by briefly treating some pertinent theological considerations of the identity crisis in the priesthood and by analyzing its organizational causes.

Theological Considerations of the Crisis

Having identified priests with the image of Christ the eternal priest by their sharing in his threefold office of preaching his gospel, celebrating his mysteries, and ministering pastoral care to his followers,[2] the council has promised them the role of leadership of a Christian community based on a renewed relationship to authority:

Priests, prudent cooperators with the episcopal order as well as its aids and instruments, are called to serve the People of God. They constitute one priesthood with their bishop, although that priesthood is comprised of different functions. Associated with their bishop in a spirit of *trust* and *generosity,* priests make him present in a certain sense in the individual local congregations of the faithful, and take upon themselves, as far as they are able, his duties and concerns, discharging them with daily care.

. . . let them so *lead* and serve their local community that it may worthily be called by that name by which the one and entire People of God is distinguished, namely, the Church of God.[3]

In cases where they are still required to serve under pastors, the council has specifically instructed these older priests to create proper professional working conditions where the former can express their ministry with trust and support:

. . . older priests should receive younger priests as true brothers and give them a hand with their first undertakings and assignments in the ministry. They should likewise try to understand the mentality of younger priests, even though it be different from their own, and should follow their projects with good will.[4]

The council has also recognized the need for the development of new roles for priests that are more consistent with contemporary culture and more productive for the mission of the church:

All priests are sent forth as co-workers in the same undertaking, whether they are engaged in a parochial or supra-parochial ministry, whether they devote their efforts to scientific research or teaching, whether by manual labor they share in the lot of the workers themselves—if there seems to be need for this and competent authority approves—or whether they fulfill any other apostolic tasks or labors related to the apostolate. All indeed are united in the single goal of building up Christ's Body, a work requiring *manifold roles and new adjustments,* especially nowadays.[5]

It is painful to admit that all priests are not united in the work of building up the body of Christ. In the recently released summary of a sociological study on priestly life and ministry sponsored by the National Conference of Catholic Bishops, it was concluded that:

Large numbers of priests are dissatisfied with the way the ecclesiastical structure is shaped and the way decision-making power is distributed; but the leadership of the Church does not share this dissatisfaction. Furthermore, it would appear that differences between younger and older priests on the distribution of power and authority are rooted in ideological differences about the nature of the Church and religion.[6]

Beset by an increasingly grave identity crisis, many younger priests wait well over twenty years before they are assigned to lead a Christian community. They frequently become disillusioned in the ministry when they fail to discover the required roles through which they can express a meaningful service to people which is significant of their own understanding of the nature of religion and the purpose of the church. Not only is their role fixed but their vocational growth is impeded by static parochial structures that confine them to traditional assignments under dominative pastors with little or no opportunity for new adjustments. In far too many instances their role is ill-defined and their career undeveloped because

of unsatisfactory authority relationships and unproductive organizational conditions.

Organizational Analysis of the Crisis

In a recent social-scientific study of the work experiences and
career growth of Roman Catholic priests of a particular diocese
conducted by Douglas T. Hall and Benjamin Schneider of Yale
University, extensive data have been uncovered that point to
the underlying organizational causes of this crisis in role identity among curates (assistant pastors). In order to properly
analyze this crisis, it is important to read the data in the light
of the theological considerations of priesthood and authority
referred to above.

By measuring the components of self-image factors among
priests, the report reveals that:

. . . the curates consistently appear to be in a less favorable
position than the pastors or specials. As a group, they feel more
dissatisfied, more underutilized, and their self-perceptions suffer
most drastically from superior-subordinate contacts. . . . We
view the criterion variables of satisfaction, self-perception and
utilization of skills as indicators of the individual's level of
personal development in his work. Therefore, we would conclude that curates as a group show a very low level of individual
development, and we have seen that this low development is
related to the type of authority they experience.[7]

By examining the characteristics of the role assignments of
priests, the Yale study alarmingly exposes the scarcity of possibilities for the career growth of curates in the present organizational system of the church. The research acknowledges
that ". . . it *is* a problem to a young priest that he has to wait
22 years before he can have a parish assignment with significant responsibility and challenge." [8] The following factors
which inhibit the psychological success of curates demonstrate
". . . *the great perceived underuse of the human potential
available in the younger priests of the Diocese*":[9] (1) they
possess extremely limited opportunities for goal challenge and
work choice; (2) while most of them are prevented from

working autonomously and from receiving any feedback on their work performance, very few enjoy *supportive* autonomy from their pastors; (3) they are frequently engaged in work not central to their concept of ministry; and (4) in such a work climate the possibilities for the attainment of their goal are considerably diminished.[10]

As a consequence of their study, Hall and Schneider conclude:

> . . . the conditions necessary for career development through psychological success are generally lacking for assistant pastors in this Diocese, although certain of these conditions are present in varying amounts for pastors and specials. Therefore, we would indicate that there are many areas in which the organization could provide improved opportunities for the growth of its priests.[11]

Summary and Conclusion

From this theological and organizational analysis of the identity crisis of the priest, it is indeed clear that his reidentity can only be re-established through the reform of parish structures which will permit more satisfactory authority relationships in the ministry and more productive organizational conditions in the church. As such, the analysis specifies that this pastoral reform must provide the priest with the opportunities for: (1) exercising an early leadership of a Christian community; (2) setting challenging goals for himself and selecting an appropriate assignment where he can work to attain them; (3) enjoying autonomy in his work through renewed authority relationships; (4) being engaged in work that is central to his concept of ministry; and (5) receiving feedback on his work performance. With the realization of these opportunities, the precise theological constructs necessary for redefining the role of the priest will be drawn and the proper organizational conditions necessary for his career development through psychological success will be established. In short, the reidentity of the priest will be secured through the pastoral reform of the church.

CHAPTER II
REIDENTITY THROUGH
PASTORAL REFORM

Interrelating the data of the above social-scientific study of the work experiences and career growth of priests with the conciliar theology of the priesthood emphasizes the need to redefine the role of the priest through the pastoral reform of the church in order to provide for his psychological success and vocational growth in the ministry and so to secure his reidentity. Both the theology and the data quite forcefully show how the role of the priest is determined by the form of the parish. Heretofore, not only priests but all Christians, save those who entered the religious life, have had but one pastoral option through which they could express their faith and mission—and that has been through the local parish. In an age when life was relatively static and confined to restricted areas of space and time, this territorial or geographical model was sufficiently expressive of a denominational Christian witness and quite effectively specified a particular parochial ministerial role. During an age when life leaps beyond the provincial boundaries of space and time, however, other pastoral alternatives sufficiently expressive of a more ecumenical Christian witness are required which specify more secular and pluralistic ministerial roles. Thus, "new adjustments" for contemporary forms of ministry imply a primary necessity to plan new forms of parish community in a mobilized society where the priest can discover the required "manifold roles" through which he can render meaningful service to God's people.[1] Such planning for priestly reidentity through pastoral reform demands a depth of vision which can only be projected through interdisciplinary perspectives.

Interdisciplinary Perspectives

Since the completion of the Yale study of the priesthood, the particular diocese in question has not provided many areas in which improved opportunities for the growth of its priests can be realized. It has adopted a rather selective approach to the interpretation of the data and has concentrated on the implementation of the conclusions of the report in the area of personnel procedure of priests' assignments. In this area an important program in team ministry and co-pastorates has recently been set up which does address itself to the problems of rank and file ministry and seniority appointments. While the program has cut back on the prolonged twenty-two year waiting period for the priest's assumption of responsibility and challenge, it has not allowed sufficient options for him in diversified ministries where he can experience his appropriate psychological success and career growth.

As a case study, it is important to uncover the pertinent underlying causes for this local church's failure to creatively respond to the Yale study. After considerable debate in the senate of priests and among the entire presbyterate over an interpretive report of the study conducted by a preliminary personnel board of the diocese, a very forward looking proposal for implementing the conclusions of the study submitted by this board was rejected. A modified plan for alternative assignments in co-pastorate teams under the supervision of a permanent personnel board was subsequently adopted and implemented. The resultant vibrations from this heated debate over personnel issues and parish reform are still being felt and continue to be transmitted to a confused people of God through the honest reporting of the distinguished diocesan weekly. From these developments, it is evident that while the clergy of the diocese is disturbingly polarized, the laity is wandering in puzzled pilgrimage.

With compassion for the bishops, priests and people of this local church, however, it should be stated that their struggles during these changing times have been disconcerting due to a lack of interdisciplinary research which could provide for them new insights into these organizational problems of church reform. Little or no work has yet been submitted on the significant interrelationship between sociology and ecclesiology as a theoretical and empirical base upon which to reconstruct the form of the parish and to refashion the style of ministry. While the Yale report and the other studies referred to in this book are indeed helpful and have been conducted with a high degree of scientific and theological expertise, they were not initiated with any formal attempt to interrelate the respective disciplines and certainly not completed with any pretenses of designing practical plans for parish reform. What is now needed is a study which recognizes that the identity crisis of the priest will be resolved neither by the pure scientific analyses of statistical surveys and interpretive reports, no matter how steeped these may be in the secular sciences of psychology and sociology, nor by the sure theological definitions of ministry, no matter how steeped these may be in the sacred sciences of Christology and ecclesiology. On the one hand, scientific studies on the priesthood have consistently missed the marks of faith, hope and love which inspire a man to devote his life in service of the corporate body of Christ, even when his psychological success may be low and his career growth obstructed. Statistics can never adequately measure these theological virtues and ecclesiological concepts that constitute the foundation of the priest's vocation to the ministry and undergird his determination to persevere in its profession. On the other hand, theological studies on the priesthood have ironically failed to acknowledge the humanity of the priest in service of an institutional church and this at a time when Christological studies have radically stressed the humanity of Christ. If these latter studies can admit the human condition of God's Son, contemporary studies must admit the human condition of his priest and the organizational conditions of his church.

So recognizing the need to apply some organizational theory

to ecclesiology can be helpful on two counts: first, it can provide a sociology for the integrative pastoral reform of the church from which practical plans can be devised to create more productive organizational conditions for the psychological success and career growth of the priest; and secondly, it can outline an ecclesiology for an integrative ministry which defines the need for more satisfactory authority relationships in the church and for a proper balance between its official and charismatic ministries. Only from these interdisciplinary perspectives which view the practical personnel problems of the professional ministry in the light of a sociology for pastoral reform and an ecclesiology for Christian ministry can the role of the priest be redefined and his reidentity refocused.

A Sociology for Pastoral Reform

The social pathological problems of the institutional church so acutely reflected in the case study of the diocese referred to above and in the indicated reports of the National Conference of Catholic Bishops are widespread not merely in the American ecclesiastical scene but abroad as well. These symptoms continue to eat into the organizational stability of the church, threatening the very foundations of institutional unity and inviting schism. To appreciate the seriousness of these ills, one has only to recall the division that has set in in the Dutch church, not to mention the thousands of priests who have left the ministry and the numbers of these who have even separated themselves from the church. In response to one of the most publicized examples of these departures, namely, the case of Charles Davis and his question of conscience,[2] Gregory Baum has recorded an incisive diagnosis into these sickening conditions and has prescribed ". . . the introduction of new social processes which open the Church to the Spirit and enable her to give up her pathological attachments to the past."[3]

While one can hardly question the need for such remedial measures, the application of new social processes to the institutional body of the church constitutes an intricately complex sociological problem which causes organizational reactions much the same as occur in the process of the organic transplants of modern medicine. Because of the biological laws of organic unity among the cellular components of a physical body, any addition of a foreign substance into that body tends to be immediately rejected. Likewise, because of the sociological laws of social cohesion among the individual groups and successive generations of an institutional body, any addition of a new social process into the organizational life of that body tends to be immediately rejected. It is not easy for any body, physical or moral, to give up attachments to the past, even if these attachments are pathological.

In psychology, Erik Erikson points to the problems of the adaptive process in individuals growing up in society confronted with personal and social change. Recognizing the evolutionary levels of life and growth, he reflects a profound respect for history, as he plots the course of the individual's life stages and resolves personal identity crises through the preservation of "ego integrity." He maintains that one does not really give up his past, even if it has been pathological; on the contrary, one builds and rebuilds his life from one stage to another and develops his potentialities while possessing the integrity of his life cycle, as he interacts with a widening social radius.[4] Applying Erikson's theories to institutions as well as to persons means that organizations and people all have an integrity of life whose order and meaning in history demand the acceptance of its past; and that when this past has experienced a pathological fallout, a new stage can be reconstructed upon its "essential strengths." Erikson's model draws a blueprint of these "basic virtues" which evolve from stage to stage and appear from generation to generation, thereby providing social cohesion for people and institutions challenged by changing systems of human and social values.

In sociology, Talcott Parsons constructs a paradigm of evolutionary change for modern societies and institutions which points the way to the integration of differentiated systems and sub-systems encountering the problems of process and change. Sensitive to the threats of polarization in social systems caused by innovators who would insist upon giving up the past, he articulates that ". . . changes do not imply that the older 'residual' unit will have 'lost function' in all contexts of its operations." [5] He cautions the innovator not to neglect other conditional factors such as the past when introducing new processes into the system.[6] He states that the primary function of the societal community is to integrate the system into a collective organization with unity and cohesiveness.[7] Parsons' model allows room for the introduction of new processes into institutions and societies and, through "adaptive upgrading," encourages those who may be pathologically attached to the past to ascend to a higher level and healthier order of commitment. In effect, his scheme, like Erikson's, utilizes the "basic patterns" or virtues of the system to preserve and to promote institutional unity and stability in the process of social change.[8]

Thus, it is impelling that when one would introduce new social processes into the institutional life of the church, he does not insist that its members give up their pathological attachments to the past. He must accept these attachments as part of the integrity of the church's life cycle and concentrate on its essential strengths in the process of upgrading its life to a higher level and healthier order of commitment. Linking these basic institutional virtues of the church through the historical course of changing times, this approach ties together the successive generations of Christians with their respective value systems. Any scheme for the pastoral reform of the church which recognizes these sociological principles of organizational theory will not only preserve the unity of the church in the process of change but will also suggest appropriate practical plans for the reconstruction of the parish as a means to create more productive organizational conditions for the psychological success and career growth of the priest. (See Chapter III.)

An Ecclesiology for Christian Ministry

As the Yale report reveals that improper "superior-subordinate contacts" have marred the self-image of priests and have contributed to their low level of individual development, its data reflect a distorted ecclesiology of Christian ministry. It is thus apparent that more satisfactory relationships must be drawn between priests and their superiors based on the New Testament concept and expression of authority. The urgency of this need is accentuated by the following disclosure from the conclusions of the sociological report to the bishops on priestly life and ministry:

There are systematic and substantial differences between bishops and priests on almost every matter we studied. In most cases, the bishops hold different points of view and positions than even the priests in their own age group. Given the disagreements over power and over appropriate reforms in the Church, these systematic differences of conviction indicate a serious and potentially dangerous "gap" between the priests and the hierarchy.[9]

The kind of authority relationships which Jesus had in mind for the church was expressed by him at the Last Supper: "You call me Master and Lord, and rightly; so I am. If I, then, the Lord and Master, have washed your feet, you should wash each other's feet. I have given you an example so that you may copy what I have done to you" (Jn. 13:13-15). From this living model Vatican II reconstructed for the hierarchical ministry a theology of authority in terms of *service* rather than dominion:

For the nurturing and constant growth of the People of God, Christ the Lord instituted in his Church a variety of ministries, which work for the good of the whole body. For those ministers who are endowed with sacred power are servants of their brethren, so that all who are of the People of God, and therefore enjoy a true Christian dignity, can work toward a common goal freely and in an orderly way, and arrive at salvation.[10]

By so redefining the nature of ecclesiastical authority and redirecting its expression through the principle of collegiality,[11] the council also restored the New Testament model of the sharing of apostolic authority among the various ministries in the church.[12] In effect, this biblical redefinition of authority calls for the restitution of the fullness of Christian ministry through the collaboration of hierarchical and charismatic ministries.[13] Post-conciliar theology compels the church to recognize the radical role distinctions of diversified offices and charisms that are an essential part of the apostolic tradition of Christian ministry and episcopal authority.[14] These distinctions in ministerial roles are crucial to the resolution of the identity crisis of the priest since they provide corrective insights into the faulty superior-subordinate relationships of the pastor and the curate and draw new lines for bridging the gap between the bishop and the priest through more proper collegial authority relationships.

According to most scholars, the presbyter-bishops in the New Testament were the elder overseers of the Christian community (1 Tim. 3:1-7; Titus 1:5-9) and eventually assumed the responsibilities of collectively exercising pastoral care over the churches founded by the apostles (Acts 20:28-29; 1 Peter 5: 2-4). With the expansion of the church into new areas and the multiplicity of pastoral responsibilities, the office ultimately split into the hierarchical form of the monarchical episcopate (one ruling bishop) and the presbyterial priesthood (his associate priests). While the office of the priest then assumed the pastoral responsibilities for the individual churches, the office of the bishop took on the apostolic character of overseeing all the churches. Thus, the leadership of Christian communities became exclusively associated with the offices of bishop and priest at different sociological levels. As such, the priest was never intended to function in the capacity of an assistant pastor; the assistant was the deacon from early apostolic tradition (Phil. 1:1; 1 Tim. 3:8-13).[15] The restoration of this important role distinction in fulfilling the responsibilities of pastoral care should help immeasurably to solve many of the present problems of the pastor-curate relationship.

Some of the problems associated with the priest-bishop relationship could likewise be resolved, were these role distinctions properly respected. In particular, modern biblical research quite conclusively shows that the office of the bishop is distinct from the New Testament office of apostleship and that, as such, the bishop was never intended to be an innovator in the church; the innovator was the missionary apostle who encountered new situations. Those charged with the responsibilities for the pastoral reform of the church would therefore do well to acknowledge the limitations of the present form of episcopacy to either make "new adjustments" or to exclusively control them.

Perhaps then it would be wise for Catholics to affirm explicitly, and not merely implicitly, that in the modern Church some of the principal activities of the Pauline apostolate, especially as regards offering leadership to face new religious problems, have been taken over functionally by men and women who are not bishops—by theologians, by enterprising priests and religious who by circumstances are thrust into new situations, and by perceptive laity with their manifold competencies. In the complexities of a modern diocese the main activities of most bishops do not and cannot take this direction. They can meet their responsibilities, however, by properly consulting with those who are involved in theology, in evangelization, in new apostolates, etc. The continuation of the functions of the Pauline apostle is the responsibility of the Church as a whole.[16]

This is not to say that the bishops should not have any authority over innovative experimentation; on the contrary, to respect the valid historical and theological developments in the authority of the episcopal office, it is equally necessary that the bishops exercise a collegial supervision over pastoral innovation in conjunction with well-prepared innovators, who may be thrust into new situations, and with qualified resource people from theology and other related socio-religious disciplines.[17]

Although the restoration of more satisfactory authority relationships for priests should help to reform their proper self-image and should help to contribute to their individual development, a more authentic ecclesiology of Christian ministry cannot be expressed without a proper balance between the official and charismatic ministries in the church. It cannot be denied that the ministerial role of priests, which has been briefly traced in the New Testament church, has been onerously overplayed since the balance of ministry was disrupted with the diminishment of the charismatic ministries of the faithful. While it is not within the scope of this work to uncover all the reasons why the specific charisma of the faithful have been relatively inactive for centuries, it nevertheless seems important to acknowledge that the major causes for the deactivation of their charismatic ministries are more sociological and political than theological. With the spread of Christianity into various geographical areas and the consequent development of the parochial foundation of churches governed by a monarchy of bishops and served by a presbyterate of priests, the clerical caste system of a hierarchical ministry was established. This system, of course, had evolved from earlier species of clerical ministry in hierarchic Judaism.[18] However, in post-Judaic Christianity, the responsibilities of ministry were expediently assumed by the hierarchy of the clergy for practical purposes. Christian mission then became the exclusive prerogative of ordained clerics for political purposes. Unordained Christians eventually became deployed of their ministerial rights and privileges with the consequent silencing of their charismatic gifts.[19] With the faithful so slighted, their segregation from the clergy in the missionary activity of the church has, in effect, divided the unity of ministry and has confined its practice to the jurisdictional limits of canonical orders and to their corresponding institutional forms and styles. Because of this distortion to the one ministry of Christ, clerical ministers have been impaled with an identity crisis in their profession and the church impaired with an organizational crisis in its mission. The resolution of these crises demands the resetting of the balance between the official and charismatic ministries of the church for the sake of restoring the ecclesiological integrity of Christian ministry.

Summary and Conclusion

Recognizing the need to apply organizational theory to ecclesiology for the purpose of planning for priestly reidentity has provided a sociology for the integrative pastoral reform of the church and has outlined an ecclesiology for an integrative Christian ministry. As these interdisciplinary perspectives have illustrated the importance of preserving institutional unity in a changing church, they have also defined the need to create more satisfactory authority relationships for priests and to reset the balance between official and charismatic ministries.

Upon this theoretical base, a practical plan for the pastoral reform of the church can now be designed as a means to create more productive organizational conditions for the psychological success and career growth of the priest. From this design, a redefinition of his role in the church can be formulated for his reidentification in ministry.

CHAPTER III

A SOCIOLOGICAL PLAN

FOR PASTORAL REFORM

In order to systematically design a practical plan for the pastoral reform of the church as a means to create more productive organizational conditions for the practice of ministry and for a new identity in its profession, it is first necessary to analyze the organizational conflicts which are contributing to the identity crisis of the priest. This analysis will help to locate the institutional tensions in the church that are pulling apart the members while dividing and weakening their missionary endeavors. The analysis will also help to assess the threats of this polarization process provoked by those pathologically attached to the past and by those disruptively detached from it. Because of these functional problems of differentiation in the system of the church and the corresponding need for an integrative plan for their resolution, the sociological theories of Talcott Parsons alluded to above seem best suited to work the analysis and to construct the plan.

A Sociological Analysis

According to Parsons, the organizational conflicts of any institution can be adequately resolved by respecting "four independent functional imperatives": *adaptation, goal-attainment, integration* and *latency*. While an organization operates according to an institutionalized value system, it nevertheless is subject to constant external and internal pressures to change its values. These pressures arise from two primary sources of

25

change, namely, cultural and motivational. The former are those sources which originate from outside the organization's value system and impel some members, adopting other values because of external cultural influences, to change this value system. The latter are those sources which originate from inside the organization's social structure, giving rise to certain internal motivational tensions among some members to rebel against particular institutionalized role expectations. As these two sources of change generate the organizational conflicts of an institution, they, in effect, challenge the latent values of its "pattern maintenance" (structures) and its "tension management" (authority). Thus, the most important functional imperative relative to the organization's stability is latency. In the stress of these system problems arising from these two sources of change, the organization's efficiency is restricted and its institutional unity, resisted. As the functional imperative invoked to relax these strains, integration seeks to maintain solidarity among the diversified units of membership and to promote operational efficiency. The two remaining functional imperatives, adaptation and goal-attainment, are set in motion by the conflicts arising out of the organization's interchange with the external environment and its situational conditions respectively. The adaptive function is responsive to the problems provoked by the process of differentiation in the environment and enables the organization to grow as it encounters change. The function of goal-attainment permits the organization to control the environment by synchronizing the confronted situational conditions with its strategy for gratification. This general theory of Parsons, usually signified as his AGIL scheme, shows how these four functional imperatives can maintain equilibrium in an institution and insure its continued existence and growth in spite of its organizational conflicts.[1]

Using this AGIL scheme of Parsons as an analytical base, it is possible to outline the organizational conflicts of the institutional church and to illustrate how its system problems can be resolved through *structural adaptation, goal substitution* and *integration* with respect for its *latent religious values*. While this use of Parsons' scheme assesses the internal and external organizational needs of the institutional church and measures its adaptive capacity for coping with the problems of social change in the external environment, the design is not focused on the church's "ability to change the environment to meet the needs of the system," as Parsonian usage would dictate,[2] but on its ability to change the system to meet the needs of the environment, as conciliar tutelage would indicate.[3] The church, unlike other institutions of society dependent on economic gratification from the attainment of their goals, exists for the disinterested ministerial service of society. As a social institution engaged in evangelization for the attainment of ultimate spiritual goals, it operates according to the principle of adaptation and therefore must change its system, whenever necessary, to include the substitution of more immediate temporal goals in order to insure its missionary gratification. The purpose of the scheme, then, is to construct a fundamental sociological framework for parish reform through which the church can acquire a more transcendent social identity in an institutionalized missionary enterprise.[4]

Structural Adaptation.   As traditional parish structures tend to contain the church within the confines of its own residential interests, more committed Christians recognize the need to adapt these structures in order to maximize the church's relationship to the external environment and to mobilize its resources for the more mission-oriented goals of serving the distressed of society. With some already involved in adapted forms of Christian community, these people frequently commit themselves to the apostolate within the organization through a variety of movements and "outside" the organization, if necessary, through the underground. In effect, those who remain within the institution are more often than not suspect of their liberal persuasions and labeled as "litniks" or "ecumaniacs." Those who are forced underground are isolated from the main lines of communication in the church or, at worst, separated from its fellowship by excommunication.

Goal Substitution.   Because of the economic strain and

institutional weight of parochialism and its self-containing goals, perceiving Christians are beginning to question the values of their attainment. As these people become more aware of the secular implications of the church's mission and more sensitive to the immediacy of human suffering and want, they begin to substitute more relevant goals that are capable of responding to the urgency of the situation. By engaging themselves in the civil rights movement, the peace movement, the youth movement and the like, they are determined to change the system, political as well as ecclesiastical, to meet the needs of the people. They are convinced that by adopting the goals of these movements they can be a more meaningful sign of hope in the eternal to those struggling in the despair of the present. They insist that this sign can be most forcefully expressed through the socio-political dimensions of mission. In effect, these Christians are often disturbingly dismissed as social or political activists and at times reproachfully condemned as "communists."

Latent Religious Values. Threatened by new forms of structural adaptation and by old fears of secularized goals, the more conservative Christians are stabilizing into their "protective" congregations determined to preserve their latent religious values. Older people, unable to relate secularization to their beliefs, tend to suspect church renewal, fearful of losing the continuity of tradition and their dependent religious identity. The "pattern maintenance" function of the traditional form of the parish and the "tension management" function of the expected role of the priest relax the fears created by renewalists and protect them from the external pressures of cultural change. In effect, these Christians are all too often written off by renewalists as having nothing to contribute to the modern church and not too infrequently neglected by insensitive innovators who fail to transmit the treasures of tradition to the young.

Clothed in the garments of social change, the youth are consequently unable to relate tradition to contemporary life styles and counter-cultural values and are incapable of identifying in the dormant congregations of their parents. They are thus tending to abandon all institutional forms of the church, with some seeking new religious experiences through a variety of natural and transcendental means.

Integration. Sensitive to the problems of the young and the old, of liberals and conservatives, more moderate Christians prefer to work within the system to effect needed change. Careful not to disregard the latent religious values of their conservative confreres and cautious to apply the "adaptive upgrading" innovations of their liberal associates, these Christians are committed to preserve the unity of the church and to insure its effectiveness in mission. In effect, though they may be in the best position to bring about solidarity and efficiency in the institutional church through their integrative efforts, they are seriously handicapped by a lack of hierarchical support and leadership and by a need for a sustained and systematic plan for responding to change.

While the hierarchy of this country may be unresponsive to these organizational conflicts in the church, as one could safely conclude from the data uncovered in the above-mentioned reports and from the recent critical analysis submitted by Father Andrew Greeley, chairman of the National Conference of Catholic Bishops' subcommittee on sociology,[5] it should, in all fairness, be admitted that the bishops likewise suffer from a need for a scientific plan for responding to change in the church. One of the most familiar fallacies that they and others committed to the integrative imperative are fooled by is that change in the system must be implemented gradually. For an age characterized by the phenomenology of rapid social change, the slow implementation of change in the church can be disastrous. This fundamental point is beyond question and is well-marked by the socio-religious problems of racial and cultural alienation that have erupted in the church and in society in the short years of the sixties. Slow change has cheated not only priests but all Christians and all people as well. What is needed therefore for the particularly pressing problems of polarization in the church is a sustained and systematic plan for responding to rapid social and religious change carefully designed to pre-

serve the unity of its membership and to enhance the efficiency
of its mission.

A Sociological Plan

Incorporating the four independent functional imperatives of
Parsonian theory into an ecclesiological design, the following
sociological plan for the pastoral reform of the church is proposed to resolve its organizational conflicts. This plan is also
presented as a means for creating more productive organizational conditions in the church and for preparing the setting for
the integrative practice of Christian ministry. First, it should
increase the church's missionary efficiency by providing a multiplicity of ministerial roles for the priest through which he can
experience psychological success and career growth. Secondly,
it should establish the proper conditions in the organization for
the reconstitution of collegial authority relationships through
which the balance between official and charismatic ministries
can be reset. Based on the AGIL scheme of Parsons, the plan
contains various specific models of parish community which
are designed to effect the structural adaptation, the goal substitution and the integration of the local (diocesan) church
with particular sensitivity for the latent religious values of older
priests and parishioners. Four sets of models are described
representing different forms of church community in a variety
of local situations. A brief delineation of the specialized role
of the priest in each model set with an evaluation of some
crucial functional aspects of the set relative to the ministry is
also drawn as an outline from which conclusions can be formulated for his role redefinition and career growth in the priesthood and for his new identity in the ministry.

Models of Structural Adaptation

Employing the functional imperative of structural adaptation,
the following set of models would open the church to the wider

interests of society and would maximize its relationship to the external environment. These models would expand the missionary activity of the church and would mobilize its ministerial resources to include the previously inactive charisms of the faithful. In addition, the forms of Christian community shaped by these models would attune the church to the council's admonitions by engaging the priest in ministerial "work requiring manifold roles and new adjustments."

The Floating Parish. This form of Christian community would be based on the New Testament concept of fellowship or fraternal communion in Jesus Christ expressed as a "Way" of life (Acts 9:2; 18:25-26; 19:9,23; 22:4; 24:14,22) in the breaking of the bread, in the gospel mission to society and in common prayer (Acts 2:42-47). By following this "Way," the members would realize strong bonds of mutual concern for one another and would extend this concern to the poor in selected areas of various mission activities. In addition to serving the material needs of the afflicted, they would occasionally break the bread of the eucharist with them in their homes and comfort them with God's saving word. They would also celebrate the eucharist together on Sundays wherever the community might be engaged in a specific mission project. During the week, the members could follow the early Christian practice of offering morning and evening prayer in common when assembled for committee work or missionary assignment; otherwise they could so adapt this primitive custom as to observe it in private as a daily inspirational means of communal interaction.

The membership of the community would be open to anyone desirous of giving witness to this "Way" of the Christian life. Its size would be determined only by the effectiveness of communication and collaboration among the members.

The Commune. With the advent of the new ethics and its emphasis on personal and provident responsibility through free and creative responses to human situations [6] and with the widespread changes in cultural values and life styles among the younger generation, some Christians might be called to give witness to gospel values in this context through the commune. In this form of Christian community, the members would be enabled to enter into deeper interpersonal bonds of mutual concern, likewise based on Acts 2:42-47. "The faithful all lived together and owned everything in common" (v. 44). The members could express this "Way" of the Christian life in a semi-monastic style insofar as they would partake of meals in common and would daily observe specified hours for common prayer according to a convenient schedule. They would appropriately adapt this style, however, to contemporary social patterns of work and leisure and religious modes of worship and mission. They could, for example, frequently break the bread of the eucharist together in their home and cooperate in various missionary projects through local community organizations. From time to time, they could participate in the liturgy of the neighboring parish and help with its apostolate. They could also enjoy membership in a floating parish or in other forms of community which might be complementary to their ways of witness.[7]

It would be especially significant that these Christians express their "Way" of life openly both in traditional cultural areas and in counter-cultural settings. In the former area, the customary monastic expression of hospitality could be most effectively extended to local parishioners by opening guest rooms with invitations to participate in this "Way" of life for selected periods, a gesture which would immeasurably help to reduce suspicion and to confirm the genuine character of such a style of the Christian life. In the latter setting, a redeeming sign of the "Way" could be witnessed, through similar strategy, to some adherents of the counter-culture who are wandering in their search for authentic values.[8]

The Pentecostal Community. The distinct form of this community would be charismatic in the biblical sense of 1 Cor. 1:4-9; 12:4-11. Although charisms as gifts of the Holy Spirit are for the whole church (1 Cor. 12:12-30), they would be regulated in this community through special meetings of prayer

(1 Cor. 14:26-40). While these diverse gifts would be given by the Spirit for the inner peace and strength of the community (1 Cor. 14:26,33), they would open the members to his power (Acts 2:1-13) inspiring them to build up the body of Christ in the service of the apostolate (Eph. 4:7-12). Inasmuch as the gifts would often be manifested by intense religious experiences, such as prophesying and speaking in tongues, they would require some spiritual direction and pastoral supervision, especially for the service of mission. In this regard, it would be wise for the members to heed the admonitions uttered by Paul that these charisms should always be utilized for the benefit of the community and the edification of the people (1 Cor. 14:3-5, 12,19,26).

Appearing as the conclusion of a lengthy discourse on the nature and purpose of these charismatic gifts in the body of Christ, these admonitions accentuate the importance of the community's preserving unity with the universal church. For these purposes the place of the liturgy in the Pentecostal community could be most efficacious. Not only could the celebration of God's word and sacrament be an integrating ecclesial experience in worship; it could also provide the wisdom and the grace for cooperative involvement with the local parish in witness.[9]

The Servant Parish. In neglected areas stricken with poverty, racial injustice and other such social evils, the church could obediently fill its biblical role as "suffering servant" (Is. 42:6-7; 50:4-5) by the formation of a community placed at the service of the poor.[10] Operating out of a storefront in a strategic inner city location, the community would be comprised of members inclined to express their Christian commitment through social work. A limited staff of full time social workers would conduct such necessary services as food collections, emergency housing, legal aid and referrals. This staff would also be responsible for enlisting volunteers from suburban parishes or from other communities to serve the poor as members of the mission.

The characteristic difference between this operation and

other social service agencies of community organizations is that the servant parish would form a worshiping community. Its main purpose would be to convey a living sign of hope to oppressed people and to alleviate their sufferings. Thus, in conjunction with the social service activities of their mission, the members would frequently celebrate their hope in Jesus Christ through the eucharist and other forms of prayer either in the storefront setting or in the homes of the people.

The Ecumenical Parish. In areas of concentrated interfaith activity where religious, educational, social or political concerns are shared, such as in university, medical or legislative centers, the ecumenical parish could proclaim a needed missionary sign of ecumenism to all churches and religious bodies. With the increasing possibility of a solution to the problems of intercommunion, this kind of parish could be constituted as a eucharistic community through which families of interdenominational marriages could jointly practice a common Christian faith. With this image, it could fulfill a more consistent ecumenical role in a pluralistic society through common worship and joint involvement in Christian social action.

The ecumenical parish could be productive of more effective pastoral strategy with which ministers and priests could share a common official ministry. It could, for example, provide new possibilities for campus and hospital ministries designed to serve the people in a more communal context than is possible through the traditional chaplaincies. Moreover, it could provide a desperately needed change in the ministerial strategy of the military whose chaplains are so often prevented by present government channels and ecclesiastical structures from exercising the prophetic office of their ministry.

The form of the ecumenical community would vary according to the degree of fellowship and the intensity of commitment among the membership. It would also be dependent on the permanent or temporary association that the members might have with the community itself or with the particular institution to which the community might be attached. More often than not, however, a plurality of forms, as described in these proposed models, could be serviceable in one given area and could co-exist with a more traditionally structured residential parish. In this latter setting, the bishop could invite his Protestant and Orthodox episcopal colleagues or the corresponding proper authorities to appoint a minister and priest to assume the co-responsibilities of official ministry with his appointed priest. By extending the principles of collegiality and reciprocity to embrace other offices of authority and other forms of ministry, such a gesture would indeed open new ecumenical directions in the common quest for Christian unity.

Professional or Occupational Communities. Certain associations of profession or occupation which bring together related groups of Christians in a stable, quasi-stable or even transient manner could offer a truly responsive sign of Christian life and ethics to the social, economic and cultural orders with the establishment of parish communities structurally adapted to the work of the profession or occupation. Professional or occupational communities could be formed accordingly for such groups as doctors, lawyers, public officials, merchants, workers, actors, etc., to enable them to experience the sustaining support of a eucharistic gospel fellowship in the face of increasing stress from the complex social and ethical issues of their work. Communities of this type could supply profound resources for their members in their professional or occupational moral dilemmas and could assist them to make a significant missionary impact on society as well as on their particular profession or occupation.

As an example of this, a kerygmatic form of Christian community could be developed with a repertory theater company. Through the medium of religious and secular drama, the theater troupe traveling and performing as a community of artists dedicated to gospel values could reach appreciable numbers and influential segments of the silent majority. With such a prophetic purpose, the community could be set up in any given resort area to perform a series of plays composed to speak out on the social and ethical implications of current issues. Through the contacts of interested tourists, the community could arrange for off-season tours to various local areas throughout the country. Because of the interdiocesan and ecumenical nature of this mission, the community could be co-sponsored by the National Conference of Catholic Bishops and the National Council of Churches, whose services could be utilized for any necessary spiritual or pastoral direction of the work.

Living perhaps in the form of the semimonastic commune, the community itself would be a sign of faith and hope to the contemporary theatrical world, so many of whose artists perform amid personal and professional struggles against faith and hope. It would, at the same time, be a sign of love and acceptance of other playwrights and actors who, through the media of the arts, are also responding to God's mission in the secular.[11]

Role of the Priest in Structural Adaptation.   Inasmuch as the priest is called to the leadership of a Christian community, the casting of his role in these adapted forms of parish would involve the necessity of acknowledging the specific *role distinctions of leadership* in the personal and communal ministry of the faithful and the public and pastoral ministry of the priest. These distinctions would allow the faithful to resume their privileged place in the ministry by utilizing and coordinating their personal charisms in communal mission for the common good of the church. They would thus undertake the *charismatic leadership* of the community and would assume the responsibilities of determining its missionary strategy as well as providing for its temporalities. This leadership could be entrusted to an elected board of directors who could fulfill these responsibilities through committee assignments. These distinctions would also allow the priest to assume his proper role of *pastoral leadership* in the community through the fulfillment of the public functions of his cultic, prophetic and ministering offices. By his cultic office, he would unite the community in the eucharistic body of Christ and to the universal church (1 Cor. 10:16ff.) and would reconcile the members in their internal disputes as well as in any external estrangement from the unity of God's people that they may suffer in wandering from the truth. By his prophetic office, he would proclaim this truth through the preaching of the word and would direct the community by this word that its public image may always conform to its biblical image. By his ministering office, he would provide for the spiritual care of the community, counseling its members, consoling the disturbed, comforting the sick and through a variety of other services, such as his own prayer, suffering and "ordinary work." [12] In this pastoral capacity, the priest would bear the ultimate responsibility of leadership in the community, for, by this threefold apostolic office, he would be commissioned by the bishop to oversee the preservation and development of biblical tradition in the community and the building up of its body in Christ.[13] The delicate balance between the charismatic leadership of the faithful and the pastoral leadership of the priest would be maintained by mutual respect for the particular charisms and offices of their interrelated ministries and by the common charism of love in their ministering service. "It is only in the objective exercise of ministering love, of which not only wide knowledge but also discrimination and tact are essential components, that charismatic gifts can be safeguarded against abuse." [14]

The multiple forms of parish community developing from structural adaptation would often demand a plurality of ministerial roles from the priest enlisting not only the services of his pastoral office but his personal charismatic gifts as well. These roles could be filled through several appointments on a full or part-time basis determined by the particular form of the community and the personal charisms of the individual priest. For example, a priest could be assigned to work with a repertory theater community on a part-time basis while serving in other forms of parish. He could even be assigned on a full time basis if he happens to be a playwright or an actor, thereby more directly incorporating his "ordinary work" into his pastoral office.

These manifold roles would maximize the priest's missionary relationship to the external environment and would extend his ministry into areas of the secular hitherto untouched by the traditional style of the parish priesthood. So, expanding the pastoral boundaries for the priest, these roles would enable him to serve the widely diverse needs of people living and working in a pluralistic social order. The diversity of these roles would, moreover, provide him with abundant opportunities to make the "new adjustments" in ministry required by Vatican II for a changing church in a mobilized world.

Evaluation: Structural Adaptation and the Underground. There is no doubt that in some sections of the church these kinds of adaptation to traditional parish structures would be met with some degree of opposition. In many instances, the strength of such widely accepted intra-organizational movements, as in ecumenism and in liturgy, could provide the necessary resources for implementing these changes. In other instances, however, it might be imperative for the priest, so convinced of the urgency for adaptation, to take the community underground. In the event that this strategy would be required, it should be remembered that this extra-organizational adaptation could be an enriching experience for the whole church inasmuch as the priest and people committed to this radical stance for church reform would paradoxically manifest a new sense of loyalty to the church precisely for courageously acting as catalysts for change in spite of the personal and professional risks involved. It would be important in these cases to open the fullness of the priest's historical perspective that he might view the temporary record of "disobedience" in the light of true tradition and in the vision of responsible faith. It should be stressed that so electing this course of church reform for higher motives than blind obedience (for which there is ample precedence in the New Testament and in church history) would not only be responding to the needs of numbers hoping for more liberating ways to celebrate their faith but would often help him to realize a new sense of freedom in his own work. This position could enable him to explore new roles of ministry in less clericalized forms. By force of sheer monetary imperatives, he would have to seek a secular occupation requiring a different ministerial life style and a more common place of residence. In a recent progress report of its study on the life and ministry of the priest, the theology subcommittee appointed by the National Conference of Catholic Bishops acknowledged the need for such changes:

"Clerical culture" refers to a sociological texture woven of distinctions and privileges which set priests apart from American society. Its multiple strands are constituted by the dependence on rectory living, clerical garb, titles, isolated seminary education, exemption from military service, preferential treatment, and most of all, by celibacy. Those priests who value such a life-style should be free to pursue it as they see fit, but those who do not should be equally free to relinquish it. Priests gratefully acknowledge that many of these privileges have been accorded them by a generous and well-meaning laity, but the priests' deep concern for that same laity prompts them to put aside a distinctive "clerical culture" in order to serve others more effectively.[15]

These changed conditions for ministry would be more consistent not only with the present socio-economic patterns of life and work but also with possible future psycho-social patterns of multiple professional commitments.[16] Hence, in addition to increasing the possibilities for the priest to extend his ministry through a plurality of organizational relationships, the benefits that could accrue from this exploratory adaptation in different ministerial life styles would hasten the day for the declericalization of the ministry and the debureaucratization of the church.[17]

Models of Goal Substitution

By substituting other goals that are more secular in nature and more universal in need than traditional parochial goals, the following set of models would enable the church to respond more efficiently in contemporary Christian mission to urgent situations inadequately served by traditional parochial forms. In this way, these models could open the church to new experiences of parish through the dynamics of a movement. According to Gregory Baum, a movement is defined "by its

mission or function in the wider community to which it belongs." He insists that "the sociological model for understanding
the Christian church today is 'the outer-oriented movement.'" [18]
He further states that "the Church as movement would intensify
the people's involvement in the life of society. Through con-
versation and common action, the Church would draw men
more deeply into the mystery of redemption present in human
life." [19] As such, the communities presented in these models
would frequently involve the borrowing of certain ideologies
like those of the peace movement, the civil rights movement or
the anti-poverty movement and theologically endorsing them
with a faith commitment that would entail an intensified involvement in social action through a self-sacrificing gospel
service to humanity. The structural form of these movements
in terms of Christian community would vary widely depending
on the nature of the substituted goals and the kind of ideological or political organization in concern. For example, communities, collectives or communes could be formed in a given
location by those engaged in community organization work, the
peace movement or the youth movement.

The Vista Collective.   The whole concept of Vista could
have been conceived from the pages of the New Testament.
It represents a true and contemporary expression of secular
mission. However, volunteers who would prefer a close structural identification with a form of Christian communal mission
in the secular could group together in a collective within which
they could live or at least share together some material goods,
such as food, an automobile or motorcycle and other utilities.
They could invite people with whom they work and whom they
serve to participate in the collective in relative degrees depending on the frequency of their association and the intensity of
their commitment. The members could occasionally worship
together in their homes or in other suitable places of their
work and express a common witness through careful and relevant strategy for Christian social action. Such an approach to
this secular mission would indeed strengthen the ties among

the workers and could even instill in them a deeper and stronger commitment to the voluntary service.

The Shalom Community. A great missionary service to violent America could be rendered by Christians united in community through faith in quest for national and international peace. Committed to a just, political and social reform through non-violence and sustained by the spiritual support of communion through eucharist and common interaction, these peacemakers could express a more effective sign of peace by organized communal witness than by the often isolated efforts of individual draft card burners and other conscientious objectors. In this respect, the supportive bonds of community would be immeasurably sustaining to certain members who might feel called to risk imprisonment or other punitive sanctions for necessary, conscientious violations of civil law. Moreover, as the community would share many common interests with more militant groups and would seek their many related goals, it could conceivably influence some revolutionaries, through exemplary strategy and action, if not through dialogue, to select more appropriate means for revolution which more faithfully conform to the principles of Christian social ethics.

The Sanctuary. The highly successful rehabilitative efforts for drug addicts by those involved in youth work or in the counter-cultural movement could draw the church "more deeply into the mystery of redemption present in human life." This work, basically counseling in nature, would intensify the Christian's "involvement in the life of society," were the church willing to form therapeutic communities for drug addicts and for those engaged in drug work. Respecting the alternative modes of therapy for drug prevention and treatment, various communities could be established to serve the diverse needs of those addicted to drug use. The sanctuary, for example, could take the form of a crisis intervention center where those who may be "tripping" could find comfort, care and reassurance. With the staff forming the nucleus of a Christian community, provisions could be made for occasional common worship and for open group discussions on the religious aspects and transcendental implications of drug use. The sanctuary could thus offer some enduring spiritual motivation to drug abusers along with its therapeutic hospitality. This approach to drug work could attract the addict to return to the sanctuary regularly by enlisting from him a commitment to the service of other addicts in need of his help. Such a fresh experience of his sense of personal dignity and value in relation to his membership and service in and through the community could provide the necessary crutch for continuity in the rehabilitative process of his permanent cure and health.

Role of the Priest in Goal Substitution. The role of the priest in these forms of Christian community would generally revolve around the prophetic office of his ministry. By his response to lead the particular movement in the proclamation of the gospel message to the wider community, the priest would often have to replay the biblical role of the prophet to remind politicians of their duties to change the system to meet the needs of the people and the nation. Ever conscious of the admonitions of Jesus the prophet who changed the system of the sabbath to meet the needs of men (Mk. 2:27-28), he would frequently be called to express his commitment in an exemplary manner of self-sacrificing service to reverse any sinful social or political conditions confronted (Mt. 23:13-39). At times, heroic witness might be required of him, as has been the case with Father Groppi and the Berrigans (Phil. 1:12-14); but, more often than not, his prophetic office would be utilized for the purpose of leading the members of the community in reconciling the wider community and its political leaders to the New Testament goals for justice and rights and for peace and love.

The cultic and ministering functions of the priest's office would be fulfilled in accordance with the particular communal form that the movement would take. His role of leading the community would, in general, be expressed according to the distinctions made above regarding charismatic and pastoral leadership.

Evaluation: Goal Substitution and Politicization. Inasmuch as these movements are usually related to networks of national organizations and, as such, are independent from the church regarding their nature and purpose, their existence and their mission in Christian community would, in large measure, be self-determined. These various situational factors could, as a matter of course, present some problems for the official church in terms of ideological politicization and hierarchical conflict. Substituted goals could, at times, be contrary to the normally accepted policies of the ecclesiastical authorities. These difficulties, notwithstanding, could be resolved in most cases by a specialized and tactful priest who could not only provide the spiritual insight to properly relate the ideology of the substituted goals with the theology of missionary goals but who could also guide the members of these movements to assume personal, communal and ecclesial responsibility for their activity vis-à-vis the ultimate accountability of the bishops.[20]

Models for Respecting Latent Religious Values

With the changes introduced into the church through the adaptation of its structures and the expansion of its goals, the following models of Christian community would represent the most important forms for its organizational stability. Designed to respect the latent religious values of more conservative Christians, these models would preserve the basic form of the territorial parish and stablize the traditional role of the parish priest. The preservation of latent values and the stabilization of the ministerial role, however, would not anchor the people and the priest to the past but would provide for them in the familiar grounds of these models the necessary foothold for their response to rapid social and religious change.

Local Parishes. Since not all Christians are endowed with the same charisms and hence not called to the same degree of missionary involvement, local congregations would still represent the ordinary form of parish. Respecting the natural groupings of people in given areas, local parishes could furnish genuine expressions of close worshiping communities oriented toward the universal community of all men. Accessible to every ethnic, racial, occupational, professional and age group in this latent form, these parishes *could be* meaningful signs of the catholicity of the church and incentive aids to project attitudes to universal realities. Through more serviceable structures of diocesan, regional and parish councils, they could open the needed channels of interparochial communication and collaboration in the apostolate, thus avoiding the narrow enclosures of parochialism. Restrictions in membership would be determined only by the preservation of efficient communication, especially in worship and in witness, and of personal ministerial service. Such small parish congregations would be unencumbered by the conservatory weight of institutional holdings and financial burdens and would be individually staffed by a priest, a deacon, married or single, and two sisters free to do ministerial work, hopefully as deaconesses.

Role of the Priest in Respecting Latent Religious Values. Although the role of the priest in the local parish would be somewhat structured along traditional lines, the ministerial goal of forming genuine Christian community, as redefined by the council [21] and as underscored by a reduction of boundaries and administrative duties, would allow for a greater emphasis on his pastoral leadership. With the establishment of a parish council which could assume the full responsibilities of the charismatic leadership of the parish, as suggested above, the priest would be in a more favorable position to concentrate on developing real pastoral leadership in the community. With the assistance of the deacon and the sisters and the cooperation of appropriate committees of the parish council, he could devote full time to creating gospel fellowship in the parish. Close to the people through his ministering visits, he could sustain them in the insecurity of their confusion over changing values and of their fear of changing forms. By so "tending" the "management" of his ministry in the conventional role expected by his parishioners, he would be a personal help to them in building their trust and a supportive sign to them for preserving their latent religious values. By so "maintaining" the "patterns" of this ministerial style, he would, moreover, provide the necessary framework for their identification in familiar congregational forms. In the meanwhile, his exposure to current developments in theology through a continuing professional education center [22] and to local developments in pastoral reform through the diocesan and regional councils, would hopefully incite him to more actively prepare his parishioners for the values of church renewal.

Evaluation: Latent Religious Values and Transition.   During this period of transition, it would be crucial that the latent religious values of the more conservative parishioners and the older priest be respected. By conserving the basic form of the congregation, the local parish would not only permit such people to find sufficient coherence for self-identity in coping with the socio-religious problems of church reform, but it would also provide the proper setting through which their exposure to developing religious values and changing pastoral forms could be redeeming. Through the retention of his role as pastor, the older priest would continue to find a customary work climate which would be so necessary for continuity in his work performance as well as in the preservation of his self-image and role in the ministry. Older parishioners would likewise continue to find a comfortable parish climate in their "protective" congregations which would be so necessary for continuity in the preservation of their faith values and their hope through the waning years. However, by so reordering its ecclesial priorities at the expense of its institutional and economic values, the local parish could be redeemed of its pathological attachments to the past. Moreover, by so reassessing its latent religious values, the local parish could inspire its congregation to redevelop its parochial structures into more communal forms through which its priest and parishioners could experience together the integrity of collaborative Christian ministry in their official and charismatic roles. In such a therapeutic climate where the rich soil of tradition could be cultivated by the seasoned gardeners of the faithful, newer forms of pastoral life could grow into young offshoots for contemporary mission. In a church so protected by these latent models in whose congregations dormancy would be metamorphic rather than paralytic, no Christian would have to be written off by anyone.

Models of Integration

As the keystone to organizational unity, the following set of models completes the archway upon which the continuing work of pastoral reform would be constructed. Supportive to the structural components of all the other forms of Christian community, these models would consolidate the membership of the local (diocesan) church and conjoin its ministerial work. They would constitute the structures through which bishops, priests and people could efficiently collaborate in their common missionary task of building up the body of Christ.

The Sectional Parish. Respecting the sociology of community in its pluridimensional forms of the family unit, the neighborhood group, the congregation, and the general community, the larger parish could more readily create Christian fellowship by individually sectionalizing into smaller communities at the level of the neighborhood group. Each section could be assigned to a priest who would act as pastor of the community and would be totally responsible for its pastoral care. During the week, intense concentration could be given to the development of communal spirit and action within the section through liturgical and pastoral programs in homes and neighborhood centers. Informal gatherings for home masses and discussions could be organized on a regular schedule at these locations, drawing the family into the communal bonds of the neighborhood. On Sunday, the priests and people of each section would assemble at the congregational level in the parish church to observe the Lord's Day without distinction of their respective sections, thus manifesting a visible sign of the unity of the whole worshiping community.

The administrative work and charismatic leadership of the sectional parish would be entrusted to a sectional council whose elected representatives would in turn serve on the larger parish council. Delegates from this council would comprise the membership of the regional and diocesan councils. The purpose of these multiple level councils would be to coordinate the work and mission of all the neighborhood sections and to promote the unity of the congregational parishes and the diocese.

Finally and by way of an example of a unified diocese collaborating in the work of the apostolate as a servant church, an interdiocesan network of cooperative parish mission could be established within the framework of the multiple level councils. Through this network, the neighborhood section and the congregational parish could then project their common concerns and efforts into other deprived sectors of the larger diocesan and secular communities.[23] These interconnecting ties would strengthen the ecclesiology of the neighborhood and the congregation since the residential character of these levels of community not only insulates suburbanite Christians from the concentrated areas of need in which they are called to serve but actually isolates urban Christians into segregated areas of need from which they are called to emerge.[24] In this context, the designation of a particular urban ghetto as a sectional parish with a full-time priest would indeed help to awaken its inhabitants with hope and to remove the "stone" away from their "tomb."

The Team Parish.   In larger parishes unable to be sectionalized, Christian fellowship could still be achieved through a team approach to ministry which would incorporate the services of priests as co-pastors, deacons as assistants, and sisters and the faithful as mission workers. A balanced expression of official and charismatic ministries in a more traditional setting, the teamwork would include programming for the social apostolate as well as for domestic and congregational liturgies. These programs would be coordinated in the regular sessions of the parish council composed of the ministerial team and of adequate representation from different age levels of the parish. They would be planned to respect the pluridimensional forms of community mentioned above and would be implemented according to the distinct ministerial roles of the team. These efforts could be facilitated especially through the council's participation in the diocesan and regional network of councils.

Role of the Priest in Integration. Insofar as the plan for pastoral reform employed in the integration models has been designed to break down the larger parishes into more manageable sociological units, the priest's prime target in serving these units through his pastoral leadership would be the small family-neighborhood group. At this nuclear stratum of society, he would find the appropriate psycho-social conditions where his hearers could be favorably disposed to hear the gospel message of Christ and to respond with intent.[25] Celebrating the liturgy and sharing the word in this context,[26] he could instill in them a corporate sense of the Christian life and form with them a corporate team for Christian mission. Following up this communication by personal contact with his ministry of pastoral care through home visitation, he would be closely associated with families, with youth and with the poor, the sick and the aged. His role with these people would be to project them from the introverting traps of loneliness and isolation to the wider ranges of community and universal concerns. Through his particular association in the various councils on which he would serve and through his actual contacts with other families in cooperative parish mission, he could make this projection a realized experience for them in terms of mutual visitation or personalized spiritual interaction.

Another crucial form of priestly service in these kinds of parishes would be the integrative role of reconciling the old and the young. Since it is precisely within the confines of the congregation, the neighborhood and the home where the generations clash, the priest would have to be prepared to experience numerous conflicts from the mixture of these diverse groups at each level of the parish. The old would seek him out for reassurance and stability; the young would look to him for support and identity. He would, in effect, be frequently cast in the role of reaching out to both generations in these difficult times of transition. His outreach, however, would be a constructive and rewarding experience in building up the body of Christ. Through this role, the priest would help to preserve the solidarity of the community and to promote the missionary efficiency of its members.[27]

Evaluation: Integration, Church Unity and Missionary Efficiency. Inasmuch as the specific purposes of the integration models would be to preserve the unity of the church in the total range of pastoral reform and to increase its missionary efficiency, evaluating these models would involve the explanation of just how these objectives would be achieved. Since almost all efforts for structural adaptation and goal substitution would necessarily take place within the geographical areas of the traditional parishes or their sections, priests assigned to these integrative forms would hold the key to organizational unity and cooperative ministry. Rather than regarding the emergencies of these newer forms as competitive threats to their parishes, they would look upon them as associate enterprises in the common missionary work of the church.[28] With such an attitude of trust and acceptance, they would be in a position to develop an *exemplary consciousness* among their parishioners by encouraging them to regard the members of these innovative communities as committed Christians called to a specialization in the apostolate. By extending the parish facilities to the members of these communities for their mission projects and by promoting dialogue between them and their parishioners,[29] the priests would also create a congenial climate where collaboration in mission could be achieved. In the event that numbers of their parishioners would feel called to join these communities or to form new ones as a result of this exposure, the priests would then be in a position to reform their parishes in conformity with the smaller latency models where Christian community would be more viable in a less mobilized context.

Evaluation of the Plan

Integration, Episcopal Leadership and the Institutionalization of Change

While missionary efficiency would undoubtedly be promoted with the collaboration of the official and charismatic ministries of Christians, the integrative efforts to achieve solidarity in the church within the total range of pastoral reform, as suggested by the above sociological plan, would ultimately depend, however, on the support of its episcopal leadership. No longer constituted on the vertical lines of a top-heavy authority base, this leadership would itself enjoy the horizontal support of its members who, through their cooperative ministries, would share in the decision-making responsibilties of church polity in accordance with the theological principle of collegiality. In this kind of hierarchical system, the bishop would be cast in the role of a *superior coordinator* charged with the administrative responsibilities of integrating the specialized and diversified ministries of the four model sets into the one ministry of Christ. In such a capacity, he would no longer be isolated from priests and people but, as an engaged leader, would be supportively involved in their integrative efforts as well. Through the collegial process of leadership, the bishop would be relieved of the burdens of overly centralized responsibility and absolutized accountability. He would thus rescue the polity of the church from the narrow confines of organizational task-performance and system-maintenance, sharing through collegiality its policy determination with his priests and the faithful. In this way, he would serve to equalize the official and charismatic ministries of the church, charging them both with sharing the responsibilies of adapting structures and expanding goals. Acting as the chief integrator of the diocese, he would supervise the coordination of these adapted structures and substituted goals with the latent religious values of the church.

When, for example, an innovative form of Christian community is born in his diocese, the bishop would father this child in his ecclesial family, even if it were unwanted. He would be actively engaged in caring for its support, especially by communicating its needs to the other members of the diocesan household. As an episcopal father, he would be in a strategic position to create a basic compatibility among the members of this household and could easily interrelate their various ideologies and goals. Inasmuch as this household contains a hierarchical sub-system in the presbyterate, it would be imperative for the bishop to open the lines of communication between this neophyte community and the pastors of the area in which it was born. By preparing these priests and their parishioners for this structural change, the bishop would set the pace for the process of adaptive upgrading and would create the harmony for an exemplary consciousness. These harmonious relationships could be most favorably formed were the bishop to visit the new community with several of these pastors offering his cooperation and sealing its trust by personally presiding over some of its liturgies. So inviting the confidence of the new community and so enlisting the active support of the more traditional parishes, the bishop would initiate the integrative imperative and would utilize his episcopal office to coordinate its organizational functions for the purpose of consolidating the work of pastoral reform in his diocese.

In such an integrative setting, the constitution of collegial authority relationships would be sealed and strengthened by the interdependence and specialization of official and charismatic ministerial roles among the hierarchy and the faithful.[30] In the end, the organizational conditions created by this kind of episcopal leadership would not only be productive of an integrative practice of Christian ministry but would, moreover, be promotive of the psychological success and career growth of priests.

While this sociological plan for pastoral reform would offer the church a flexible system for collegial authority relationships in the integrative practice of ministry and more productive organizational conditions for the priest,[31] it would also introduce a desperately needed system for the institutionalization

of change in the church and in the ministry.[32] As both the
Fichter and the Schallert-Kelley studies revealed, the church
and the priest are sociologically and theologically conditioned
by the continuity of social and religious change.[33] On this
account alone, it is the responsibility of the church to provide
an institutionalized system through which the priest can creatively respond to the continuously changing demands of his
ministry by making the required role adjustments without
renegade sanctions. In such an integral system as represented
by the above models, the church would be in a position to
handle change much more efficiently and positively. While it
might not be able to officially approve every innovative ex-
periment of the underground movement, it would be sufficiently "agil" to maintain at least unofficial communication
with its innovators. Through this kind of integrative dialogue,
the official church could learn from its continued openness to
review the unapproved experimentation while the underground
could be encouraged to reassess its position in view of the
common good of the universal ecumenical church.[34]

Summary and Conclusion

The application of the AGIL scheme of Talcott Parsons to the
system problems of the institutional church has suggested a
practical sociological plan for its pastoral reform. According
to this plan, four sets of models of Christian community have
been proposed for a church in a mobilized society with a
variety of pastoral alternatives in each set through which
priests, together with the faithful, could express a particular
style of Christian witness in diversified forms of official and
charismatic ministries. Designed to restore the balance between
these complementary forms of ministry, these models would
promote the development of an *exemplary consciousness* for
faith and mission among all Christians, thus fostering ecclesial
solidarity and missionary efficiency. By so creating an integrative ecclesiology, these models would also produce a diversity of interdependent and specialized roles in Christian

ministry shared harmoniously by the priests and faithful and coordinated collegially by the bishop. As this plan would integrate the differentiated systems and sub-systems of the institutional hierarchical church, it would invite the bishop to assume a more engaging episcopal leadership as a *superior coordinator* and to prepare his priests and the faithful to positively encounter the problems of rapid social and religious change. While it would give the church the required "agility" to introduce new processes into its systems through adaptive upgrading, it would respect the evolutionary process of change and would provide for its institutionalization. Moreover, building on conciliar directives, this plan would open to priests manifold secular and pluralistic roles for contemporary ministry and would encourage them to make new and necessary adjustments in their professional careers. In these integrative ecclesiological models and their productive organizational forms, priests could begin to redefine their role in the church and could hope to realize that degree of psychological success needed for their vocational growth in the ministry. Through this sociological plan for pastoral reform, they could indeed acquire a new identity in the priesthood.

CHAPTER IV
A NEW IDENTITY
FOR THE PRIEST

It has to be admitted that the foregoing sociological plan for the pastoral reform of the church designed as a means to resolve the identity crisis of the priest remains, at this point, in the realm of theoretical speculation. Although the plan has been submitted with a description of the specialized role of the priest in each model set accompanied by an evaluation of the functional aspects of the set as these would relate to the practice of ministry, this description and evaluation have been prognostic, not diagnostic. What is now needed for the practical and determinative resolution of this crisis is the implementation of the plan over a sustained period of time followed by another social-scientific study testing the work experiences and career growth of priests serving in these models. Short of this long-range approach and in want of its tested results, what can be attempted, however, is to examine how the proposed sociological plan redefines the role of the priest in a plural world and promotes his career growth in a reformed church. This examination should then point to his new identity in the ministry and indicate how the plan equips the church to shape his new image.

Redefining the Role of the Priest

The descriptive and evaluative speculation formulated from the framework of the sociological plan does posit a sufficiently broad base upon which the required theological constructs can be drawn to rebuild the image of the priest and to redefine his role. As a man of unity, the priest assumes an image and fulfills a role, throughout this plan, that faithfully represent the New Testament doctrine on ministry and creatively develop the teachings of Vatican II on the priesthood in the modern world. Reflecting these biblical and conciliar concepts, he is pictured as a *leader* of God's people commissioned by apostolic office to *reconcile* them to him in pluralistic settings, *forming* them into his priestly people in a diversity of Christian ecclesial communities through his word, his sacrament and his own suffering service. Redefining the priest's role then involves three terms: *leadership, reconciliation* and *building*.

Leadership. The leadership of the priest is closely designed in this plan according to the specifications of his pastoral office. It is thus distinct from but harmoniously related to the charismatic leadership of the faithful and involves the fulfillment of the cultic, prophetic and ministering functions of that office.

As a cultic leader, the priest presides over the worshiping assembly of the community he is called to serve. Specially gifted by the Spirit with a charism for leading worship and officially ordained by the bishop with an apostolic order to express this gift for a local church, he acts as the principal liturgist for the community. In this capacity, the priest is to re-present the life of Christ to the community through the year and to direct the faithful in the celebration of his mysteries through the liturgical seasons. Inasmuch as the liturgy (*leitourgia*) is the public work of the people in its strict literal sense, however, the priest must continually strive to engage the people in public worship in such a way that *their* liturgy is inspired from their own charismatic influence and bears the impression of their own authentic contributions and active participation. The particular responsibility of the priest, then, as president of the liturgical assembly, is to direct these contributions and to lead this participation so that the life of Christ and his mysteries unfold in a coherent and relevant manner through the celebrations of the church year. Thus, the priest should encourage the liturgical committee of the community to assume its rightful place to prepare the liturgy for common and festal celebrations under his direction.[1]

As a prophetic leader, the priest is commissioned by the Spirit and by the bishop to preach the word of God, proclaiming his truth to the community for its mission to society.[2] His leadership is to direct the community by his preaching so that its public image may always conform to its biblical image. This particular ministerial goal is an extremely difficult one to attain with the reactivation of the charismatic influence of the faithful and with their active participation in the liturgy. To this end, whenever other members of the community enjoy the prophetic charism to witness God's truth to society and to proclaim its message in and through the worshiping assembly, the priest should welcome this inspired involvement from his brothers in Christ. However, since his prophetic ministry is charged with a collegial authority as well as with a mature spirituality and a developed theological training, his artistic expertise is to blend the sharp accents of this truth and to provide the exact contrast for its proclamation, especially where some of the "minor" prophets may color its message with their tones. Within the community, this leadership is not always discharged with comfort, but it must always be expressed with love, for it is only through the common expression of this charism that the order of men and the peace of God can be maintained (1 Cor. 14:32-33).[3] Within society, this leadership is not always discharged *sans reproche,* for it is not only the biblical record which gives witness to the rejection of prophets (Mt. 5:12; 23:34-36; 1 Thes. 2:14-16); it is also the juridical record that gives testimony to the fact that they are sometimes convicted as political criminals.[4]

As a ministering leader, the priest is called to serve all of God's people in the community and in society as well. He is to respond to their needs, providing for their spiritual care, counseling them when they are confused, consoling them when they are disturbed and comforting them when they are sick. While his work in these areas requires the knowledge of professional training, it more importantly demands the wisdom of a cultivated spirituality. His leadership role as a spiritual therapist will be most effective when it is fulfilled as a suffering servant (Is. 42:6a-7; 50:4). As the Lord and Savior used his wounds to heal the sickness of sin, the priest must use his personal sufferings to heal the pains of people (Is. 53:4-5). Showing how ministry moves beyond professionalism, Henri Nouwen carefully opens this personal side of the priest:

. . . the minister, who takes off his clothes to wash the feet of his friends, is powerless, and his training and formation are meant to enable him to face his own weakness without fear and make it available to others. It is exactly this creative weakness that gives the ministry its momentum.[5]

This spiritual therapeutic process gains its greatest momentum when the priest interrelates the sufferings of all those to whom he is ministering and, in union with his own, joins them to the suffering body of the mystical Christ throughout the world (2 Cor. 1:3-7). In this way, not only does he direct the faith and love of his brothers in Christ to universal realities (Col. 2:1-5), but he projects their hopes to an eternal life in the risen Christ (Col. 3:1-4).[6] Through this kind of spiritual interaction the priest is sensitized to the needs of all those whom he meets and seeks to be an authentic sign and a personal agent of hope to them. Through the spirit of the glorified Christ, he is liberated to extend his missionary search for relevant ministering activity into unexplored areas of gospel service, which may involve "ordinary work" in the secular world. Fr. Nouwen challenges the modern priest to undertake these explorations:

. . . more than ever it may be possible to experience the Spirit of Christ as a living Spirit who makes it possible to break through the boundaries of our imprisoned existence and makes us free to work for a new world.
   But this way of the transcendental experience is a way that requires ministry. . . . It calls for Christians who are willing to develop their sensitivity to God's presence in their own lives, as well as in the lives of others, and to offer their ex-

periences as a way of recognition and liberation to their fellow men. It calls for ministers in the true sense, who lay down their own lives for their friends, helping them to distinguish between the constructive and the destructive spirits and making them free for the discovery of God's life-giving Spirit in the midst of this maddening world.[7]

Reconciliation. While the ministry of reconciliation is common to all Christians,[8] especially as seen in the goal substitution and integration models of the above sociological plan, the priest, as a man of unity, possesses special reconciliatory powers from the sacramental orders of his pastoral office. As in his leadership role, the powers of this reconciliatory role are expressed through the cultic, prophetic and ministering functions of that office.

In the liturgy, the priest acts as the principal agent of reconciliation through his cultic functions of presiding over the eucharistic mysteries, proclaiming sacramental absolution and administering sacramental unction. As a reconciling instrument of God's love, he ministers the cup of forgiveness to the community of his brothers who, at times, from the human tensions of their gospel mission, break the bonds of unity in the fellowship of their service. As a reconciling instrument of God's mercy, he publicly announces to the community the forgiveness of God and the church for any estrangement in the loneliness of sin experienced by the members. As a reconciling instrument of God's compassion, he anoints the sick bodies of his brothers disintegrating from the diseases of diminishment and unites them to the "mortal body" of Christ (Col. 1:22) [9] reintegrating the universe through his cross (Col. 1:20).

In the ministry of proclamation, the priest acts as the principal agent of reconciliation through his prophetic function of preaching the word of God. As the "major" prophet of the community entrusted by his pastoral office with the service of the gospel (1 Thes. 2:4), he preaches the apostolic word with reconciliatory power:

It was God who reconciled us to himself through Christ and gave us the work of handing on this reconciliation. In other words, God in Christ was reconciling the world to himself, not holding men's faults against them, and he has entrusted to us the news that they are reconciled. So we are ambassadors for Christ; it is as though God were appealing through us, and the appeal that we make in Christ's name is: be reconciled to God (2 Cor. 5:18-20).

Commenting on this passage, Karl Schelkle describes how the prophetic function of the priest is efficaciously related to the ministry of reconciliation:

> . . . God's action in Christ embraces both aspects, the reconciliation itself, as well as the depositing of the word of reconciliation. In this word God's reconciliation is now further actualized. By being addressed to the sinner, reconciliation is continually being achieved anew, and in this way the work of reconciliation comes to its completion. . . .
> . . . after Paul has said that the establishment of reconciliation by God is actualized here and now in the apostolic word, he says finally that the word of the apostle is the same as the word of Christ. . . . The apostle is the one who brings the word. But God reveals himself in the preaching and is operative in it.[10]

As the "major" prophet of the community, the priest fulfills his reconciliatory role of proclaiming the word in conjunction with the "minor" prophets of the community, the faithful, who, from their baptismal grace and charismatic gifts, possess a share in this role. It is, incidentally, precisely for this reason that the dialogue homily has reconciliatory efficacy. Since the reconciling power of the priest and the faithful is not limited to the cultic expression of proclamation in the homily, the priest, in union with the faithful of the community, works at the prophetic functions of reconciling sinners to God whenever he proclaims the word through mission in the wider community. Moreover, since the word of God may be proclaimed in a multitude of ways, the priest can, at times, be an effective agent of reconciliation, along with the faithful, by engaging in such prophetic missionary endeavors as marching in protest groups and fasting for peace.

In his ministering service, the priest acts as the conjoining instrument of reconciliation through the crucial labors of a suffering servant (Is. 49:5a). By his ministry of the cross, he reconciles people from the restriction of sorrow and pain, from the isolation of time and death and from the segregation of change and life, drawing them into an interacting convergence with the historical, the universal and the mystical Christ.[11] It is, moreover, only through this suffering service of the cross, which he must experience himself, that he can effectively respond to the problems of polarization within the church. "And when I am lifted up from the earth, I shall draw all men to myself" (Jn. 12:32).

Building. Redefining the role of the priest from the above models of Christian community in terms of building is obviously a question of redressing the administrative functions of the pastorate in its present role expectancies. However rooted and secure the church may be in a given place by the material structural components of a "parish plant," the role of the priest cannot be defined by any valid set of theological constructs in terms of the construction of parochial buildings. On the contrary, the interdisciplinary specifications drawn from the proposed plan for the pastoral reform of the church have set these constructs for building in terms of the formation of a priestly people. This role of the priest is likewise fulfilled through the cultic, prophetic and ministering functions of his pastoral office.

From the liturgical resources of the church and upon its sacramental system, the priest is able to construct a "spiritual house" within which "the People of God" can abide. By means of the sacrament of baptism, he lays the ecclesial foundations of this house upon Christ as the "cornerstone" onto whom he sets the "living stones" of its inhabitants. By means of the liturgy of the eucharist, he enables these believers, "set apart" in this house as "a royal priesthood," to offer "spiritual sacrifices" (1 Peter 1:21–2:9).[12] This kind of house building redefines the role of the priest as a *community builder* charged with the task of forming God's people into diversified units of ecclesial worshiping communities, as indicated in the above plan. For example, in the latency or integration models of the plan, the priest could more effectively build Christian community at various demographic levels of the parish through an organized program of domestic and congregational liturgies celebrated to reintegrate the unity of baptism and the eucharist. Preparing for and celebrating the eucharist in small neighborhood groups where he would meet the expectant parents of the parish, he would be in a position to favorably dispose them and their neighbors for a deeper understanding of the corporate and ecclesial significance of the coming births of the children. He then could encourage the neighbors to take an active part with the parents in the preparation for the baptism of the children by anticipating some of the preliminary rites of infant baptism in the homes of the respective neighborhoods. By so involving the neighbors in the expectant joys of childbirth and in the preparatory ceremonies of baptism, the priest would be forming an ec- clesial worshiping community with firm domestic and neigh- borhood roots. In turn, he could place the living stones of the smaller neighborhood groups in the congregation by in- viting the neighbors to accompany the parents and their newborn infants to the parish church to assume the honors of communal sponsorship. In this role as community builder, the priest would interlock these groups as ecclesial keystones for the larger parish community by means of a congregational celebration of baptism within a eucharistic liturgy.[13]

Both in this cultic range as well as in his missionary field, the prophetic voice of the priest possesses a formative pro- jection. By preaching the word of God in the liturgy and by announcing it in his mission, he forms community among his believing hearers. This proclamatory function of the priest's prophetic ministry enjoys a sacramental efficacy inasmuch as the message actually effects what is audibly proclaimed:

Since the word as God's word is creative . . . it does not merely demand what the admonition announces, but at the same time realizes it. . . .
The proclaimed word creates the church not with a force that cannot fail, but only where it is heard and accepted. . . .
The word creates for itself its community. It has its power

from him and in him by whom it has been sent—and it still
abides in him when it is released by him.[14]

Thus, community building occurs not by means of a magical
process but by means of a faith dynamic through the Spirit.
It is this same Spirit who, at providential times and proper
places, moves the prophet to build community integratively
and, whenever necessary, reintegratively at the expense of
condemning and reforming inserviceable structures:

. . . valid preaching exists only in and through the church.
Only where there is a church is the true word spoken and
heard. Therefore it may well be possible or necessary at some
time to condemn and reform uses or abuses of the church by
recalling the biblical word and using it as a norm.[15]

It is, of course, precisely through the above sociological plan
for pastoral reform, which at times recalls the biblical word
and uses it as a norm, that the priest can fulfill such a prophetic and integrative role as a community builder.

Finally, through the ministering capacity of a suffering servant, the priest works once more as an integrative community
builder (Is. 49:5a). Like the Lord, he utilizes his own personal sufferings to form the church from his cross;[16] and so
with Paul he can say: "It makes me happy to suffer for you,
as I am suffering now, and in my own body to do what I
can to make up all that has still to be undergone by Christ
for the sake of his body, the Church" (Col. 1:24). Commenting on this passage, *The Jerusalem Bible* states:

Jesus suffered in order to establish the reign of God, and anyone who continues his work must share this suffering. Paul is
not saying that he thinks his own sufferings increase the value
of the redemption . . . but that he shares by his sufferings as a
missionary in those that Jesus had undergone in his own mission. . . . These are the sufferings predicted for the messianic
era . . . and are all part of the way in which God had always
intended the Church to develop.[17]

Developing the church as a community builder through

suffering service is not a ministry prompted by a masochistic psychology of man but by an ascetic theology of the cross. It is this theology which enables Teilhard de Chardin to speak so positively of human suffering. For him the cross is not merely a penitential experience of expiation for sin but a constructive instrument for the mission of building the universe for God and of unifying all things in Christ.[18] This creative ministry of Christ is discharged through the energy and force of love which inspires a priest to say with Paul: "Yes, I want you to know that I do have to struggle hard for you. . . . It is all to bind you together in love and to stir your minds, so that your understanding may come to full development" (Col. 2:1-2). Ministering the cross to his brothers in such a positive and formative way, the priest can direct the spirituality of the community to its full development and thus enable its members to interact with one another in all their sufferings through the bonds of love.

As the above threefold redefinition of the priest reconstructs his biblical and conciliar image, it specifies his official roles in the ministry for his missionary service in a reformed church and to a pluralistic society. Describing his image as formed by the cultic, prophetic and ministering functions of his pastorate and outlining his profile in the setting of the charismatic ministries of the faithful, it depicts these roles in terms of leading Christian community, reconciling God's people and building Christ's body. This multiple role redefinition is further complemented by the lines of relationships that the priest enjoys with all of God's people:

The priest stands in relation to many people, all of whom contribute to his definition. He is related to Jesus Christ, to the entire People of God, to all men who need his help, to the immediate community he serves, to the religious men and women with whom he collaborates, to his fellow priests in the presbyterate, and to his bishop.[19]

Through the richness of these relationships within which the collegial lines of authority are set and the integral balance of ministry reset, the redefined priest can recognize his new identity in a plural world through manifold ministerial roles in an ecumenical church.

What now remains is to examine how this church is so reconstructed in its pastoral forms that it is equipped to shape the priest's new identity by promoting his vocational growth in the ministry through its more productive organizational conditions.

Promoting the Career Growth of the Priest

The plurality of ministerial roles emerging from the rich diversity in ecclesial forms so proposed in the sociological plan does indeed equip the church for promoting the career growth of the priest as a means to shape his ministerial identity. However, in order to accurately check the equipment of this reconstructed church for the purpose of determining whether the organizational conditions of its pastoral forms are sufficiently productive to promote the career growth of the priest, it is first necessary to recall the conclusions of the theological and organizational analysis of his identity crisis formulated in the first chapter. These conclusions specify that the proper organizational conditions required for the career development of the priest must provide him with the opportunities for: (1) exercising an early leadership of a Christian community; (2) setting challenging goals for himself and for selecting an appropriate assignment where he can work to attain them; (3) enjoying autonomy in his work through renewed authority relationships; (4) being engaged in work that is central to his concept of ministry; and (5) receiving feedback on his work performance. In the organizational conditions created by the above plan for pastoral reform, the priest can aggressively realize these opportunities. First, in view of the widespread demand for specialized services in the professional ministry and his corresponding specialization in training,[20] he can expect an early, if not immediate, call to the pastoral leadership of a Christian community upon ordination, having fulfilled any needed requirements for pastoral experience in preordination field work and internship. Second, with such variety in Christian communities and multiformity in priestly work, he can set challenging goals for himself in accordance with his interests and personal charisms and through the services of a diocesan personnel board select a suitable assignment, with the approval of the bishop, where he can work to attain them.[21] Third, with renewed authority relationships based on the principle of collegiality and supplemented by a strong diocesan personnel policy based on the principles of subsidiarity, consultation, competence, etc.,[22] he can be assured of enjoying a considerable amount of autonomy in his work without necessarily having to lose the support of his superiors and co-workers. Fourth, with the restoration of the collaborative relationship between charismatic and official ministries and the resultant role distinctions between their forms of leadership, he can expect to be engaged in work that is central to his concept of the pastoral ministry. Fifth, through the diocesan structures of regional and parish councils, he can have access to channels for collective feedback in his work, which process restores the right of the community he is called to serve to test his service.[23] In this kind of organizational climate where the priest can utilize his skills, enjoy satisfaction in his work and acquire adequate self-perception through his roles, he can steadily advance to a high level of personal development in his profession. In this kind of organizational church where the priest can work to systematically attain his goals and thus periodically experience psychological success, he can confidently expect to realize growth in his priestly career and so recognize a continuing development in his ministerial identity.

Summary and Conclusion

As the sociological plan for pastoral reform traces the ministry of the priest through the cultic, prophetic and ministering functions of his pastoral office, it designs the necessary theological constructs upon which his image can be rebuilt and his role redefined. Picturing the priest as a leader, a reconciler and a community builder of God's people in each of these official capacities, the plan describes his ministerial work as integratively performed through the leadership, reconciling and building roles of his pastorate. Furthermore, it allows him sufficient flexibility within the organizational conditions of the institutional church to make the required adjustments through these manifold roles so as to realize his opportunities for experiencing psychological success and achieving career growth in the ministry. By so redefining the role of the priest and promoting his professional career growth, the plan not only points to his new identity in the ministry but actually equips the organizational church to shape his new image.

Inasmuch as the plan outlines an ecclesiological system for the modern church and its priesthood by developing its pastoral resources for constituting productive organizational conditions, it embodies for the church the kind of society that Pope John had in mind when he wrote:

The society of men must not only be organized but must also provide them with abundant resources. This certainly requires that they observe and recognize their mutual rights and duties; it also requires that they collaborate together in the many enterprises that modern civilization either allows or encourages or demands.

The dignity of the human person also requires that every man enjoy the right to act freely and responsibly. For this reason, therefore, in social relations man should exercise his rights, fulfill his obligations and, in the countless forms of collaboration with others, act chiefly on his own responsibility and initiative. This is to be done in such a way that each one acts on his own decision, of set purpose and from a consciousness of his obligation, without being moved by force or pressure brought to bear on him externally. For any human society that is established on relations of force must be regarded as inhuman, inasmuch as the personality of its members is repressed or restricted, when in fact they should be provided with appropriate incentives and means for developing and perfecting themselves.[24]

With its pastoral resources so abundantly developed by the specifications of such a plan designed from sociological theory, the church can indeed provide its priests with organizational conditions sufficiently productive to promote their psychological success and career growth in the ministry. In effect, priests can be assured of assignments to positions where their human rights are respected and their personal development fostered. In these positions, they can be encouraged to act creatively from the charismatic influence of their own set purpose and decision and can thus possess the personal dignity of acting freely and responsibly. Enjoying the support of their superiors through collegial authority relationships, they can be inspired to collaborate in the ministry with their professional associates and together with them can make the proper adjustments in their ministerial enterprises to facilitate their gospel roles of leading, reconciling and building God's people in a way that modern civilization demands. In such organizational conditions, priests can, in fact, be provided with appropriate incentives and means for developing and perfecting themselves.

CHAPTER V

PROJECTIONS: TOWARD AN ECUMENICAL MINISTRY

The role redefinition of the priest would be incomplete were not certain projections concerning the ministry and its roles drawn which, by design, should help to provide him with some appropriate incentives and subsequently with continuous means for developing and perfecting his ministerial identity. These projections should be especially helpful in providing such incentives for the priest since they would acknowledge the basic Parsonian theory on the primary sources of change for institutions [1] and could prepare the church accordingly to continuously develop and perfect its own role expectations regarding the ministry. This sociological theory would identify the external cultural influences of pluralism in society and the internal motivational interests of ecumenism in denominations as the primary sources that are presently forcing the church to direct its mission to the world through an ecumenical ministry. Thus, if projections toward this form of ministry could be internally plotted for the priest in his ongoing search for ministerial identity, this endeavor would actually participate in the process of motivating him to rise above his institutionalized parochial role expectations. To this end, a redefined priesthood in terms of multiple ministerial roles and professional career growth would contain some far-reaching ecclesiological, liturgical, educational and ecumenical role expectations for the future forms of ministry in a pluralistic world and an ecumenical church.

Ministry and Ecclesiology

In order to develop and perfect the role expectations for priests, the ministry of the Christian priesthood must be seen in its total ecclesiological context. From this perspective, there is only one ministry—that of Jesus Christ and his body, the church:

> There is one Body, one Spirit, just as you were all called into one and the same hope when you were called. There is one Lord, one faith, one baptism, and one God who is Father of all, over all, through all and within all.
>
> Each one of us, however, has been given his own share of grace, given as Christ allotted it.
>
> . . . And to some, his gift was that they should be apostles; to some, prophets; to some, evangelists; to some, pastors and teachers; so that the saints together make a unity in the work of service, building up the body of Christ (Eph. 4:4-7,11-12).

As such, the ministry does not belong exclusively to any particular group of clerics or charismatics; it belongs to the whole church. Current ecclesiology underscores this conclusion with a missiological interpretation of the doctrine of biblical election:

> Membership in the Church is a sublime vocation. Men are elected by God to become affiliated with the Christian community so that they might share the task of giving explicit witness to what has happened, what is happening, and what will happen in history. The Christian is the one who must publicly attest to his faith in the Lordship of Christ, that all human life and history make sense because Jesus is Risen. And the Christian community has the unique responsibility of announcing this fact to the world, of committing itself to the task of bringing about the Kingdom of God here and now, and of showing others what it really means to live in Christ.
>
> . . . Membership in the Church confers a responsibility and a mission.[2]

As seen, this mission is granted to individuals in community by the Holy Spirit for public order through hierarchical ministry or for private or communal purpose through charismatic ministry. Heretofore, the clerical appropriation of the ministry by the hierarchy offset the balance of ecclesiology in ministry and succeeded in suppressing the ministries of the faithful, not to mention the activities of the Spirit. By respecting the proper role distinctions of offices and charisms, as outlined in this study, the channels for the participation of the faithful in the ministry of the church will be reopened and the balance of ecclesiology reset.

With such an integral and ecclesial reordering of ministry, the hierarchy and the faithful will hopefully be responding to their specific role expectations for gospel mission in a much more unified fashion through community worship and witness. Bishops and priests will no longer be expected to be set apart from the people but as their public leaders in the pastorate will preside over their liturgical celebrations and will coordinate their missionary occupations at different sociological levels of Christian community. Emerging as leaders from the people through biblical and democratic elections,[3] they will divest themselves of their cultic, prophetic and ministering superiority of standing above the people before God as intermediary figures of exemplary holiness. They will rather assume a more theologically accurate role of standing *with* the people as their presidents and coordinators, re-enacting with them, in the corporate body of Christ, his one mediating ministry. Chosen from among the people (Heb. 5:1), they will identify with these people in community, guiding them to participate in various liturgical, educational and ecumenical phases of this one ministry.

For a more contemporary expression of the ecclesiology of an integrative ministry, as demanded by modern civilization, the role distinctions between hierarchy and people will no longer be drawn by clerical barriers at the expense of ministerial unity but by professional ties for the expertise of ministerial efficiency. It must be remembered that the radical meaning of the word "clergy" in Greek signifies "inheritance" (*kleros*)[4] and was commonly used in the New Testament and early patristic writings to denote the inheritance of all the faithful.[5] Thus, in these writings, the words "clergy" and "laity" (*laos*) described the same people,[6] namely, the faithful among whom the "lots" of ministry were apportioned by office (Acts 1:26) and by charism (Eph. 4:7). In the early church, the separative effects of clericalism were actually unknown, since the New Testament ministry was, so to speak, declericalized. It also must be remembered that the earlier meaning of the English word "professional" was not intended to convey an occupational means of support but a proficient source of competency.[7] In an age of professionalization, the ministry will require increasing need for more competence among its pastoral leaders. To this end, the cultic, prophetic and ministering offices of priests will be more competently filled by those exposed to interdisciplinary training in the theological, behavioral and social sciences. What will have to be avoided at all costs, however, in a professional priesthood will be the abuses of professionalism which have as much alienating effect among the people as clericalism. A declericalized ministry itself will, in turn, be a safeguard against these abuses, as this style of priesthood will preserve priests from the exclusiveness and inaccessibility of professionalism as well as from the impersonal exploitation of its commercial fees. The very purposes of the declericalized form of ministry will be to make ministers accessible to the people as their gospel servants (Lk. 22:25-27) and to disenfranchise them from the ecclesiastical economy of stipends and benefices. In a professionalized society and a pluralized culture, priests will no longer need to be dependent for their support and livelihood on the feudalistic offerings of the people. Through their multiple professional roles, they will extend their ministry into the secular with the utilization of their own occupational skills and charismatic gifts and here earn their living on a pivotal, relevant or peripheral basis.[8] An appreciable number of them will serve concurrently as pastoral leaders of several communities, in accordance with the diversification of the particular communities and the specialization of their own ministries, with their psychological success and career growth dependent on eschatological values and organizational merits rather than ecclesiastical dollars (1 Peter 5:1-4). Through such an authenticity in professional ministry, priests themselves will be more personally efficacious signs to people searching for authentic life styles and selfless service.

Congenial to this declericalized life style, priests will no longer be expected to remain celibate, so choosing this role only if they are blessed by the Spirit of love with its charism. Moreover, they will be free to serve in the priesthood, if they are blessed by God with the graces of the marriage state, which, by now, needs no proof, scriptural or otherwise, to establish its compatibility with official ministries.

Balancing the ecclesiological scales of Christian ministry necessarily includes a consideration of the role of women in the priesthood. One simply cannot hope to restore the integrity of official and charismatic ministries in the church, let alone the balance of their distinct roles, if he fails to acknowledge the imbalance of the sexes within the hierarchical scales of official ministry itself. In their progress report referred to above, the theology subcommittee appointed by the National Conference of Catholic Bishops courageously testified against this imbalance when they concluded that ". . . there are no scriptural or dogmatic arguments against the ordination of women to the priesthood, and in fact, some theological and pastoral reasons for doing so." [9] With a covenant that wills so much to womanhood, especially with regard to her equality in the church, women own a biblical birthright to priesthood through their baptism in the body of Christ (Gal. 3:27-28). Though they have been deprived of this right since the origins of Jewish Christianity by the early ethnic influence of a Levitical priesthood and since the development of Gentile Christianity by the later cultural caste of a clerical priesthood, they will assume their lawful roles to official service in the ordained priesthood through the counter-cultural influence of women's liberation. Already numbers of young women are enrolled in divinity schools and theology departments of universities where, in some instances, their ministerial skills are being developed through professional training. The church will thus be forced to recognize the potentially productive roles for pastoral leadership among these women, for they will be more than adequately equipped to lead, reconcile and build Christian community in the various functional aspects of the cultic, prophetic and ministering offices of the pastorate. It will be a happy day for the church when the integrity of its official ministries is insured by the Pauline policy that ". . . there are no more distinctions between Jew and Greek, slave and free, male and female, but all of you are one in Christ Jesus" (Gal. 3:28). That day will only come, however, when the clerical policies of a male ministry are redeemed by the ecclesiological forms of a declericalized priesthood.

To enhance the development of the role expectations from a balanced ecclesiological ministry and the perfecting of the role relationships between official and charismatic ministries, it is important to consider how the harmonious function of collegial authority between the hierarchy and the faithful will be determinative of the active participation of all Christians in the one ministry of Christ. It can assuredly be said at this point that the faithful will positively respond to this kind of biblical authority from the hierarchy and will actively assume their role responsibilities in charismatic leadership, as specified above. They will gracefully share in the shaping of magisterial and ministerial policy as well as ecclesiastical polity, as if through a trust.[10] Their prophetic voice will be a communal and charismatic guide for the hierarchy of priest, bishop or pope, especially when it speaks unanimously in local, diocesan, or universal communities. It will, in turn, enable the hierarchy to rediscover the supportive ecclesial sources of divine enlightenment for the fulfillment of its role responsibilities of publicly teaching or pronouncing the needed doctrine for the church and the world on contemporary religious and social issues. Through these communicative lines of collegiality, this voice will be more attentively heard by the hierarchy, because, under charismatic influence, it will speak more faithfully of the biblical message from the experiences of human life and will respond more virtuously to the situational sufferings of this life. With such charismatic tones, this voice will be recognized by the hierarchy and, through its trust, will be expressive of an electorate in the appointment of bishops and priests to diocesan and local churches. Moreover, it will, at long last, project the free speech of the faithful into the liturgical language and educational channels of the church and into the policies of its ecumenical affairs.

Ministry and Liturgy

With Christian ministry placed in a more integrated ecclesiological context, the biblical character of the church as God's priestly people will be more effectively signified and the liturgical roles of its communicants and leaders more appropriately distributed. Christians will thus characterize the theology of the priesthood of all believers in their diversified communal forms; and as they manifest a distinctive "Way" of life in the world through their specialized roles of missionary witness, they will worship God in accordance with this "Way," freely relating their missionary works to their liturgical acts. The institutionalized role expectations of the priest as a cultic functionary will then be opened to all of God's people as a worshiping eucharistic community, with the proper distribution of liturgical roles determined by personal charism as well as by sacramental office. The development of these liturgical role expectancies on the part of the institutional church will be realized only as the restrictive rubrics for worship are replaced with an *open liturgy*.

Open liturgy, much like the term "open education,"[11] will more authentically represent the worship of a free people (Gal. 5:1) and will be celebrated by this people as a living experience in praising God (Acts 2:46-47). Its liturgical forms will induce appropriate cultic actions from the people expressive of their individual and communal missionary works (*leitourgia*) and will require a new set of liturgical role expectations from the people themselves as well as from the hierarchy. Through open liturgical forms, the people will reclaim their rightful roles to express themselves in worship not only with voice, as in song, but also through movement, as in dance. The free expression of these liturgical roles will be directed by the bishop or priest who, as president of their particular worshiping community, would incorporate the works of its members into the cultic acts of word and sacrament. This openness in liturgical worship will not mean an irresponsible abandonment of ritual or rubrics by the hierarchy; on the contrary, these forms and laws will be utilized for the precise purposes for which they were originally intended, namely, to serve as guidelines for the proper celebration and orthodox preservation of apostolic tradition.[12] The guided freedom of these formal liturgies will open into the devotional lives of the people and will foster a continuation of the celebration of life in the world through informal communal and familial liturgies and through non-liturgical observances and happenings coordinated with and expressive of their particular missionary works. Open liturgy will thus cultivate an interdependence of the liturgical and ministerial roles of Christians and will promote an abundant biblical-liturgical devotional life extending into their secular lives.

Inasmuch as these projections cast new light upon the ministry and the liturgical roles and devotional lives of priests and people alike, they also point to new directions for ministry and education.

Ministry and Education

When Christian ministry is understood in the light of an ecclesiology of biblical election and a liturgy of the priesthood of all believers, it becomes immediately clear that some radical projections for Christian education and its ministerial roles are in order. If membership in the church confers responsibility and mission, and if members are to celebrate their faith in the lordship of Jesus Christ as a priestly people, it is imperative that the ministry of education be directly aimed at those capable of a faith commitment for mission. What is sorely needed in the church, then, is a reversal of child-oriented schooling to adult-oriented learning in the context of diverse forms of ecclesial communities.[13] This reversal of priorities will imply a reordered set of educational role expectations for the ministry of Christian education which, according to the ecclesiological balance of ministry, will engage all of the faithful as well as priests and religious.

Accordingly, Christian education will revolve around the prophetic mission of the church and will involve the direct learning experiences from the pedagogy of the liturgy and from the peer group dynamics of interpersonal ministering in Christian community living. The principal resources for learning, then, will be the people themselves. First, through the experiences that they will share in the kind of open liturgy described above, not so unlike the pedagogical worship of the classical catechumenate of the third and fourth centuries, they will embody God's on-going revelation in their community as they re-enact the mysteries of salvation. Their free participatory celebration of the liturgy will constitute for them a direct personal and communal engagement with the word and sacrament enabling them to identify with the biblical characters more really and with the liturgical acts more efficaciously. Secondly, through the experiences that they will share in the interpersonal ministering of community, they will be afforded immediate opportunities for interrelating what they learn in their worship with what they encounter in their lives. These peer group learning dynamics in Christian communal living will insure them with a kind of reinforcement process not only for deepening their grasp of the truth but for increasing their commitment to love.

These alternative liturgical and communal forms will constitute the setting for what might be called *open education* in the church and will provide the structures in which the improvement of human life can be experienced.[14] As adult Christians begin to integrate their own human development with their Christian life, they will more clearly recognize their faith commitment in terms of a mission to develop human life in the world. Their religious education will thus open their understanding of mission as a way of looking at the world in view of a specifically *Christian* response. Moreover, as this learning process in human development becomes centered in the Christian community, the intricate problems of religious education for children and youth will begin to resolve themselves. Formal liturgical celebrations in worship will no longer be imposed upon those incapable of a faith commitment for mission.[15] Formal curricular studies in religion will no longer be imposed upon those undeveloped members of the church incapable of mature judgment and will be offered only in the context of comparative religious studies in adult education. Ecumenical education for pre-adults, as a way of looking at the world in view of a specifically *human* response, will be offered through the childhood and adolescent years in the surroundings of Christian community according to a developmental schedule based on the individual's own intellectual and psychological readiness for religion.[16] The ultimate purpose of this ecumenical education for pre-adults will thus be to enable them to grow through these communal structures toward a gradual awareness of the specific difference between a human response to a way of looking at the world and a Christian response. Inasmuch as the adult members of the community and, in particular, the parents exemplify this Christian response by their "Way" of life, the adolescent will, in his own time, more readily recognize the full implications of church membership in terms of a faith commitment for mission. His religious education will, in effect, prepare him for the radical choice of converting his human response to life into a Christian response. In the grace of this conversion, he will open his way of life into the "Way" of Christ to be "set apart" with his "priestly people."

Drawing these projections for religious education from the ecclesiology of biblical election and from the liturgy of the priesthood of all believers illustrates that the ministerial roles of education in the church belong to the whole Christian community and not exclusively to priests and religious. The particular role expectations for the priest in the ministry of education then will be fulfilled through the major prophetic functions of his leadership, reconciling and building roles, effectually performed in an open liturgical climate and in the cooperative context of a ministering Christian community. Gabriel Moran insists on the communal imperative for this educational ministry in these terms: "Education ought to be a process in which the whole community educates the whole community for the whole of communal life. . . . Without some form of community experience, no educational venture will be successful and an ecumenical education is doubly handicapped." [17] With the rich diversity of community forms so projected for a church renewed through pastoral reform, the ministerial roles of Christian education will be expressed as a processive learning experience in community opening all the faithful to a triply blessed venture in ecumenism.

Ministry and Ecumenism

The ministerial venture in ecumenism is indeed blessed with the threefold mission in the areas of Christian ecumenism, religious ecumenism and secular ecumenism. This mission is described by Richard McBrien as a service of pluralism through dialogue by means of which Christians open themselves to encounter with one another, with believers of other religious traditions and with those who are religiously indifferent. Identifying pluralism as "a value to be promoted and sustained," McBrien stresses the importance of dialogue among its components for keeping it "open-ended" and "living." [18] Projections for this kind of mission to pluralism and for the expectations of its ministerial roles, then, can best be made by outlining a strategy for ecumenical ministry in terms of an *open ecumenism* which will generate dialogue within and among the three specific areas of Christian, religious and secular ecumenism.

Before making these projections toward an ecumenical ministry, however, it is first necessary to comment on the role of dialogue as a means to open the ecumenical movement to a wider pluralism. Dialogue in ecumenism has all too often become weary with theological discussions on doctrinal unity and ecclesiastical polity. It can, however, be "the lifeblood of pluralism," as McBrien would claim, and project ecumenism to new horizons for exploring truth, as John Dunne would claim. Although the latter does not employ the terms "ecumenism" or "dialogue," he nevertheless maps out an exploratory journey for ecumenism along the paths of a dialogical process of ". . . passing over from one culture to another, from one way of life to another, from one religion to another" and ". . . coming back with new insight to one's own culture, one's own way of life, one's own religion." [19] The most accessory vehicle for this passing over is the disposition of a "sympathetic understanding." [20] Persistently moving toward new horizons on a "voyage of discovery," this disposition constantly opens one to new visions into truth through the experiences of "living by insight." [21] While this fascinating and creative use of dialogue promotes the intended unity of ecumenism, it respects the extended diversity of pluralism. Dunne would put it this way: "In the moment of passing over you see your oneness with other men and with God, but in the moment of coming back you see your own concreteness and individuality." [22] In this sense, dialogue is an enlightening ecumenical experience which opens Christians to one another, to believers of other religions, and to peoples of other persuasions.

Dialogue of this kind will regenerate the spirit of ecumenism among Christians and will bless the church with a strategy for an ecumenical ministry. According to this strategy, new ministerial roles will emerge in the ecumenical movement which will open all Christians to the mission to pluralism and not just ministers and priests. When Christians begin to understand the dialogue that God initiated with man as a passing over of his Son with sympathetic understanding from eternity into time and from the Old Covenant into a New Testament opening his life to a Gentile pluralism, they will recognize the ecumenical Spirit of the Father's love and the ecumenical ministry of the Son's mission. They will know how the Son shared his insights with others particularly after he returned to his Father by sending the Spirit of ecumenism into his church, enabling his disciples to continue his ecumenical ministry. Baptized into this discipleship, Christians will freely assume the role responsibilities especially of this ministry guided by Jesus Christ the exemplar of the ecumenical priesthood. In this way, they will be free to pass over into the lives, cultures and religions of other men and to come back into their own lives, cultures and traditions of Christianity with enriched insight. So experimenting with truth and with religion, they will share the discovery of their insights with all men, extending the mission of ecumenism to the universal spheres of all religious beliefs and secular concerns. Touched by the spirit of this open ecumenism and moved by its exploratory strategy, Christian ministry will thus be engaged to serve all men with the ecumenical priesthood of the universal Christ, leading them through the convergence of all religions into the kingdom of the Father.[23]

Open ecumenism will play an important role within Christianity itself, for it will only be through its spirit and strategy that integration in Christian ministry will be fully attained. In order for the fruitful expression of charismatic ministries to grow in the church, the ecclesiastical climate will have to be such as to foster the spirit of trust that comes from a sympathetic understanding and to promote the strategy of dialogue, even if it comes from speaking in tongues. When Christians open themselves to passing over to other traditions of the church with this spirit and with this strategy, they will come back to their own traditions with deeper insights into the ecumenical role expectations for their ministry. In this way, new insights will be discovered, communicated and shared among their respective traditions and will open their vision so that they will know just what kind of unity in faith to confess when they pass over and what kind of diversity in tradition to conserve when they come back. The experience of passing over and coming back will help them to enrich their ministry with the spirit of unity and the strategy of dialogue for their creative participation in the continuing process of ecumenism in the future church.

Creative ministry in the future church will require increasing participation in an ecumenical process that opens into the pluralism of other religious traditions. Christians will realize that ministry was not designed by Jesus for the proselytizing purposes of bringing all men into the church but for the missionary purposes of leading all men into the kingdom. They will know that their mission must be prepared to launch into journeys toward this kingdom that will carry them into other religions. They will pass over into these religions as if on an adventure into revelation. They will experience the living God in these different traditions as they recognize the resonance of his Word in unfamiliar scriptures and uncustomary worship. Enriched with new insights into God's revealed truth and into man's common experiences of this truth, they will come back to their own religions ready to share these experiences with others. Without renouncing the creedal and cultic traditions of their own faith on this "voyage of discovery" they will build from the common base that they share with other believers what John Dunne and Teilhard de Chardin, before him, pointed to for this age of ecumenism, namely, a religion of the future through which all men will be led to the kingdom. For Christians, this ecumenical process will be centered in Christ since they believe that he is "the first-born of all creation," the cosmic redeemer, in whom all believers will be united (Col. 1:15-20, 27; Eph. 2:11-22, 3:6). Teilhard focused his projection in this way: "A general convergence of religions upon a universal Christ who fundamentally satisfies them all: that seems to me the only possible conversion of the world, and the only form in which a religion of the future can be conceived." [24]

Conceiving a religion of the future toward which the ecumenical process is steadily evolving will require the application of the spirit and strategy of open ecumenism to the secular areas of the ministry to pluralism. Christians will see the leadership, reconciling and building roles of their mission opening more and more widely into such areas as the social, political, economic and educational sectors of public life and will attempt to serve religiously in different persons or institutions with value insights focused on immediate human and ultimate spiritual goals. Passing over into these public sectors as individuals, in some instances, and as community, wherever possible, they will identify with their secular colleagues through common interests and commitments and will share with them their own distinctive eschatological vision. So proclaiming the kingdom of God in the present to the wider community, they will come back to their smaller community more conscious of a worldview and of their ecclesial self-image as a sign of hope in the future to those pictured in that view. They will share this consciousness among themselves and particularly with their fellow Christians of the larger churches, hoping to enrich and to expand their missionary witness to the dimensions of pluralism.

When the strategy of dialogue is applied in the mission to pluralism to the areas of Christian, religious and secular ecumenism, there will necessarily be a constant interchange of ministerial activity within and among these three areas. In future forms of ministry, the minister will not be confined to isolated areas of a local Christian church, as constrained by the role expectations of parochialism; he will, on the contrary, be opened through the spirit of ecumenism to the religious and secular areas of the gospel mission, as demanded by the role expectations of pluralism. An ordained priest, for example, will discover entirely new phases of his ministry when it is enriched and expanded to a pluralistic mission. As a declericalized minister to a particular Christian community of God's people, he will extend his ministry through the strategy of open ecumenism to the religiously indifferent as well as to those of other religions, sometimes together with the community he serves and other times apart from it. Always enjoying, however, the supportive interaction of the community's fellowship, he will freely move back and forth between the personal bonds of his ministerial dexterity. His pivotal, relevant and peripheral roles will be related to the leadership, reconciliatory and building functions of his cultic, prophetic, and ministering offices. The more successfully he integrates the professional roles of his ministry in these three sectors, the more effective will the official functions of his ecumenical priesthood be. So integrating his missionary activity in the three interrelated areas of ecumenism, the priest will develop and perfect his ministerial identity in an ecumenical ministry and will promote his own career growth through multiple professional roles in service of a gospel mission to pluralism.

Developing and perfecting one's ministerial identity toward an ecumenical ministry require more than just appropriate incentives and certainly more than just the hypothetical projections that have been drawn from the ecclesiological, liturgical, educational and ecumenical role expectations of a redefined priesthood. This is a process that calls for continuous means and the interdisciplinary perspectives of theology and the organizational sciences which are pointing to the need for an institutionalized ecumenical ministry. However, because of the system problems that would be encountered in all the denominations of the institutional church which would so direct their mission to the world through such a ministry in accordance with these projections, it would be imperative to develop a corresponding sociological plan based on the AGIL model of Talcott Parsons which would draw the structural lines for the future reidentity of Christianity toward an institutionalized ecumenical church. In short, an institutionalized ecumenical ministry would require an institutionalized ecumenical church. Resolving the inter-organizational conflicts of church polity by respecting the inter-organizational functional imperatives of the respective dominations, this sociological plan would not only provide adequate means for the priest to continue the ongoing process of reidentity in an ecumenical ministry but would moreover enable the Christian church to rediscover its ecclesiological unity amid interdenominational diversity.[25] This endeavor would constitute the subject of further research and would hopefully contain the material for a subsequent volume.

Summary and Conclusion

The foregoing set of projections toward an ecumenical ministry are designed to provide some appropriate incentives and subsequent continuous means for the priest to develop and perfect his ministerial identity and to prepare the church in the conflicts of continuous change to develop and perfect its own role expectations regarding the ministry. Acknowledging from the basic sociological theory of Talcott Parsons the external cultural influences of pluralism in society and the internal motivational interests of ecumenism in the church as the primary sources of change, these projections direct the priest toward an ecumenical ministry and point out for him the precise areas in or through which his multiple ministerial roles and professional career growth can be expected to develop, namely, ecclesiology, liturgy, education and ecumenism. While the projections for ministry in these areas should help to provide some incentives for the priest to rise above his past and present institutionalized role expectations, in themselves they obviously cannot equip him with the means to emerge from these roles. As seen, the above sociological plan for the pastoral reform of the church would indeed help him to make the new adjustments required by his manifold roles for his reidentity toward an ecumenical ministry in the contemporary church. However, what would be needed for the future church is another sociological plan based on the AGIL model of Parsons which would subsequently provide the continuous means to enable the priest to develop an institutionalized ecumenical ministry in an institutionalized ecumenical church.

Meanwhile, it is hoped that this work will provide some appropriate incentives and some immediate means for the parochial priest and the institutional church to begin to develop and perfect themselves. It is further hoped that the long-suffering search for priestly reidentity will not end in the parish, even when it is reformed, but will continue in the world as a "voyage of discovery" toward the ecumenical ministry of Jesus Christ.

NOTES

Chapter I

1. See, for example, "Decree on the Ministry and Life of Priests," arts. 1, 8, 22; "Decree on Priestly Formation," Preface and art. 1; "Dogmatic Constitution on the Church," arts. 28, 37, 40-41; "Pastoral Constitution on the Church in the Modern World," esp. arts. 43, 62, 75-76, 78, 91 in *The Documents of Vatican II*, ed. Walter M. Abbott, Herder and Herder, and Association Press, New York, 1966.

2. "Dogmatic Constitution on the Church," art. 28 in *ibid*.

3. *Idem.* (italics mine); the renewed relationship to authority which generates the interpersonal association of trust and generosity between the priest and his bishop is based on John 15:15: "I shall not call you servants any more, because a servant does not know his master's business; I call you friends, because I have made known to you everything I have learnt from my Father."

4. "Decree on the Ministry and Life of Priests," art. 8 in *ibid*.

5. *Idem.* (italics mine).

6. *Study on Priestly Life and Ministry* (Summaries of the Report of the Ad Hoc Bishops' Subcommittees on History, Sociology and Psychology), National Conference of Catholic Bishops, Washington, 1971, p. 65.

7. Douglas T. Hall and Benjamin Schneider, *A Study of Work Experiences and Career Growth of Roman Catholic Diocesan Priests* (unpublished manuscript), Department of Administrative Sciences, Yale University, 1969, pp. 66 and 107. In this study specials have been designated as priests who are neither pastors nor curates but those involved in extra-parochial ministries, such as in education, in hospital chaplaincies, etc. The conclusions of this factor analysis are corroborated by those of the sociological study which reported to the bishops: "The condition of the associate pastor (curate) is poor. Job satisfaction in this group, for example, is generally lower than that of unskilled workers. Associate pastors also do not feel that they have very good relationships with their colleagues" (*loc. cit.*, p. 66).

8. Hall and Schneider, *ibid.*, p. 76; see also note 111 on art. 8

of "Decree on the Ministry and Life of Priests," in W. Abbott, ed., *op. cit.*

9. Hall and Schneider, *ibid.*, p. 74; see also the data collected by Joseph Fichter on the work capacity of priests and the use of their abilities in *America's Forgotten Priests—What They Are Saying,* Harper and Row, New York, 1968, pp. 131-134. Fichter states: "One of the most important conclusions from the present study is the widespread waste of talent among the full-time parish assistants, and the consequent restlessness and dissatisfaction among the lower-echelon diocesan clergy" (p. 207).

10. Hall and Schneider, *ibid.*, pp. 106-116.

11. *Ibid.*, pp. 115-116. Compare these conclusions with those of Fichter who calls for a complete reformation of the organizational conditions of priestly work and for the professionalization of the priest as a career man. *Op. cit.*, pp. 208-209. For an important sociological research study which analyzes some of these organizational conditions as they relate to the voluntary withdrawal of priests from the active ministry, see Eugene J. Schallert and Jacqueline M. Kelley, "Some Factors Associated with Voluntary Withdrawal from the Catholic Priesthood," in *The Homiletic and Pastoral Review,* 71:2-4 (1970-1971) 95-106, 177-183, 255-267. This study concludes: "The renewal of the Church is perhaps the single most important step to be taken" (p. 267).

Chapter II

1. While this study is directly focused on pastoral reform as a means of redefining the role of the priest and restoring the proper organizational conditions for his vocational growth in the ministry, it is acknowledged that the primary questions of pastoral reform are posed by ecclesiology—namely, what is the church? and what is the purpose of the church? In order to adequately relate this study to these questions, it is suggested that the reader consult Richard McBrien, *Do We Need the Church?* Harper and Row, New York, 1968, and Colin Williams, *Where in the World?* National Council of Churches, New York, 1963. Tracing the development of ecclesiology from biblical times to the contemporary period, McBrien questions the relevancy of a Kingdom-centered church in a pluralistic world and points to some new ecumenical directions for the secular mission of the church. Tracing the development of the parish from biblical times to the contemporary period, Williams questions the relevancy of the residence-centered parish in a mobilized world and points to some new ecumenical directions for the secular mission of the parish.

2. See *A Question of Conscience,* Harper and Row, New York, 1967.

3. *The Credibility of the Church Today,* Herder and Herder, New York, 1968, p. 96.

4. Erik H. Erikson, *Childhood and Society,* W. W. Norton, New York, 1963, pp. 247-274.

5. Talcott Parsons, *Societies: Evolutionary and Comparative Perspectives,* Prentice-Hall, Englewood Cliffs, New Jersey, 1966, p. 22.

6. *Ibid.,* p. 114.

7. T. Parsons, *The System of Modern Societies,* Prentice-Hall, Englewood Cliffs, New Jersey, 1971, pp. 11-12.

8. T. Parsons, *Societies:,* p. 114.

9. *Loc. cit.,* p. 65.

10. "Dogmatic Constitution on the Church," art. 18, in W. Abbott, ed., *op. cit.*

11. *Ibid.,* arts. 22-24 and the Addenda, pp. 97-101.

12. See John L. McKenzie, *Authority in the Church,* Sheed and Ward, New York, 1966, pp. 99-100. Although the doctrine of collegiality was defined by the council as it pertains to the hierarchical relationship between the pope and the bishops, its application in practice in terms of the sharing of responsibility in mission extends to the whole church; see "Decree on the Missionary Activity of the church," arts. 37-38 and note 97 in *ibid.* Insofar as the practice of co-responsibility in mission and in *ministry* embraces the whole church, it faithfully represents the practice of collegiality in the New Testament church; see Hans Küng, *The Church,* Sheed and Ward, New York, 1967, p. 410 and J. L. McKenzie, pp. 64-65. It should be pointed out that the practice of collegiality as extended to the whole church "does not mean that all the members of the Church have offices of authority, but that each member actively cooperates in the function of authority according to his own *charisma*" (McKenzie, p. 65).

13. See Karl Rahner, *Theology of Pastoral Action,* Herder and Herder, New York, 1968, pp. 70-77. Hierarchical ministries may be briefly described as those *offices* commissioned by apostolic succession through official ordination to those called to the public service of the church; charismatic ministries, as those operations of grace given directly through special *charisms* or gifts of the Holy Spirit to individual believers for the service of the church (p. 73).

14. See H. Küng, *op. cit.,* p. 417. For a detailed description of the biblical nature, forms and functions of the various offices and charisms of ministry and their historical development in the church, see pp. 363-444.

15. See *ibid.,* pp. 409-413. On the specific role distinction of the deacon as assistant to the priest as well as to the bishop, see

The Jerusalem Bible, Doubleday, Garden City, N. Y., 1966, Titus, 1 note b and John Macquarrie, *Principles of Christian Theology,* Scribner's, New York, 1966, p. 385. In the context of the liturgy, the role distinction between the priest as leader and the deacon as assistant is vividly illustrated in *The Apostolic Tradition of St. Hippolytus,* ed., Gregory Dix, S P C K, London, 1968 (an early third century document of liturgical texts). In this ritual, the priest is described as one who is ordained to "govern" God's people (8); the deacon, as one who is ordained "for the service of the bishop" (9). Throughout these texts, the deacon appears as an assistant to the bishop and to the priest; see, for example, 4, 21, and 23.

16. Raymond E. Brown, *Priest and Bishop: Biblical Reflections,* Paulist Press, New York, 1970, pp. 77-78.

17. See J. Fichter, *op. cit.,* pp. 203-204. For the bishop to properly fulfill his responsibilities of supervising pastoral reform, he must have access to *competent* consultants. He should therefore provide for the training of "enterprising" personnel who are professionally equipped to responsibly and creatively respond to new situations. In this context, see Edgar H. Schein, "The Role Innovator and His Education," in *Technology Review,* 73:1 (1970) 32-38.

18. See Jean Daniélou, *The Theology of Jewish Christianity,* Darton, Longman and Todd, London, 1964, pp. 346-356.

19. See George H. Williams, "The Ministry of the Ante-Nicene Church (c. 125-325)," and "The Ministry in the Later Patristic Period (314-451)," in *The Ministry in Historical Perspectives,* eds. H. Richard Niebuhr and Daniel D. Williams, Harper and Brothers, New York, 1956, pp. 27-29 and 60-61 respectively.

Chapter III

1. See *Economy and Society,* Free Press, Glencoe, Ill., 1956, pp. 16-19. The above explanation represents a fundamental exposition of Parsonian theory as it applies to the functional problems of any social system. Parsons later developed this theory to include the process of evolutionary change in organizations by illustrating how the transitional stages of systems are related to certain evolutionary universals which constitute the structural foundations of modern society. Inasmuch as his theory is primarily concerned with the internal organizational needs of systems adapting to changing environmental conditions, his work contains some important implications for the adaptive capacity of the institutional church to cope with the process of the ongoing developments in ecumenism as well as for the functional aspects of its mission to

a constantly changing society in pluralism. See *Sociological Theory and Modern Society,* Free Press, New York, 1967, pp. 490-520. (An attempt will be made in the next chapter to draw some of these implications.)

2. See *Sociological Theory,* p. 493.

3. See "Pastoral Constitution on the Church in the Modern World," art. 44 in W. Abbott, ed., *op. cit.*

4. This use of Parsons' scheme is more consistent with the critique of his theory offered by Gibson Winter in *Elements for a Social Ethic,* Macmillan, New York, 1966, pp. 206-208.

5. See "The State of the Priesthood," in *The National Catholic Reporter,* 8:16 (Feb. 28, 1972) 7-10 and 15-17.

6. See K. Rahner, *Theological Investigations II,* Helicon Press, Baltimore, 1963, pp. 217-263, esp. p. 249, no. 5, and James F. Bresnahan, "Rahner's Christian Ethics," in America, 123:13 (1970) 351-354. See also John G. Milhaven, *Toward a New Catholic Morality,* Doubleday, Garden City, N.Y., 1970.

7. The church should not be adverse to multiple parish memberships in a mobilized society. As Christians multiply their associations at different levels of a pluralistic social order, they are often in a position to become involved in various forms and degrees of common witness.

8. It would indeed be a loss as well as a grave repetition of past errors in missiological strategy to dismiss the importance and the necessity of adapting structures and methods to cultures and people. See "Decree on the Missionary Activity of the Church," in W. Abbott, ed., *op. cit.* Although this decree distinguishes between missionary and pastoral activity (6), current developments in ecclesiology would certainly tend to recognize this distinction merely in terms of strategy. Thus, with due allowances for the further important distinctions between permanent cultural conditions of nations (10) and changing cultural phenomena of generations, the message of the decree is most relevant, namely, that the church must enter into culture to "heal it," to "preserve it" and to "perfect it in Christ" (21).

9. For an objective critical study of the contemporary Pentecostal movement in the Catholic Church, see Kilian McDonnell, "Catholic Pentecostalism," in *Dialog* (Winter, 1970). While this study offers minor theological criticism to Catholic Pentecostals, it emphasizes the value of their restoring genuine religious experiences in the church and recommends that "bishops involve prudent priests to be associated with this movement."

10. See "Dogmatic Constitution on the Church," art. 8 in W. Abbott, ed., *op. cit.*

11. The importance of the church's recognizing other forms of

mission than its own cannot be stressed enough in an age of pluralism. Its failure to do so has often alienated large sectors of the artists' community. For a helpful discussion of the church's relationship to the world of the arts and its responsibility to the artist, see "Pastoral Constitution on the Church in the Modern World," art. 62 in *ibid.*, and C. Williams, *op. cit.*, pp. 92-97.

12. This term refers to any auxiliary secular occupation in which the priest may be engaged. See R. Brown, *op. cit.*, p. 29.

13. See H. Küng, *op. cit.*, pp. 436-442 and Ernst Kasemann, *Essays on New Testament Themes*, S C M Press, London, 1964, pp. 63-94. Neither Küng nor Kasemann develops the potential role distinctions in leadership between the priest and the faithful, as suggested here. While Küng places strong emphasis, in the context of discussing apostolic succession, on the leadership of the priest in the community through his public office of pastoral ministry, he does acknowledge the need for the church to be "open to other and different possibilities" for apostolic succession and pastoral leadership, "such as existed in the New Testament church" (p. 442). As Kasemann outlines the relationship of charismatic ministries to office in the New Testament church, he shows some of the differences that existed, claiming that in the Corinthian church Paul "set his doctrine of charisma in opposition to the theory of an institutionally guaranteed ecclesiastical office" (p. 84). It would therefore seem that the role distinctions in leadership, as herein presented, give some recognition to the Pauline Corinthian tradition within the present Roman Catholic tradition. Moreover, the different possibilities for new relationships in pastoral leadership contained in these proposals, modeled on the New Testament church, would seem imperative if the contemporary church is to responsibly reach out to numbers of Christians who *are* serving with charisma in experimental communities *without* the leadership of a priest.

14. E. Kasemann, *ibid.*, p. 77.

15. *The Systematic Theology of the Priesthood* (Progress Report Summary), United States Catholic Conference, Washington, 1971, quoted in *The National Catholic Reporter*, 7:26 (Apr. 30, 1971) 12, no. 7.

16. See Warren G. Bennis, "A Funny Thing Happened on the Way to the Future," in *American Psychologist*, 25:7 (1970) 595-608. In Bennis' forecast of organizational forms and professional relationships, it may not always be possible or even desirable to hold with Brown that "ordinary work" should not be "a primary occupation, perhaps, but . . . auxiliary" (*op. cit.*, p. 29; see note 12 above). Like the charismatic Christian, the declericalized priest would not have to make the distinction between ordinary work and ministerial work. All work would be mission oriented. The

only useful distinctions would be acquired from organizational theory and could be applied, for strategic purposes in ministry, to the work involved in the priest's multiple organizational or other professional commitments. Bennis, for example, draws three distinct sets of role relationships which will enlist a plurality of commitments to various organizations: "pivotal" (more or less permanent), "relevant" (temporary) and "peripheral." He claims that a person who would be pivotal to one organization could have a variety of relevant and peripheral roles in other organizations (pp. 606-607). With the restoration of the charismatic ministries of the faithful, the specifically distinct responsibilities of the ordained priest in terms of the cultic, prophetic and ministering functions of his pastoral office would be fulfilled in accordance with these multiple organizational role relationships without any categorical allotment of official ministerial work to primary or auxiliary occupations. (See below, pp. 130 and 157-160.)

17. For an ecumenical perspective on some practical problems and possible solutions associated with structural adaptation in the Orthodox, Protestant, Anglican and Roman Catholic traditions, see the replies of Athenagoras Kokkinakis, Hebert Roux, Stephen Neill and Johannes B. Metz to "Does Our Church Need a New Reformation?" in *Post-Ecumenical Christianity,* ed., H. Küng (*Concilium,* vol. 54), Herder and Herder, New York, 1970, pp. 58-91. For an imaginative forecast of some possible future forms of a declericalized ministry and a debureaucratized church, see Ivan D. Illich, *Celebration of Awareness: A Call for Institutional Revolution,* Doubleday, Garden City, N. Y., 1970, pp. 69-94.

18. "The New Ecclesiology," in *Commonweal,* 91:5 (1969) 124.

19. *The Credibility of the Church Today,* p. 208. Inasmuch as Baum would recommend the outer-oriented movement as *the* sociological model for pastoral reform, he does not allow sufficient room for other Christians in the church who may not be able to identify with his political ecclesiology.

20. In a hierarchical system where the authority relationships are drawn through the horizontal lines of a collegial order and where policy determination is shared by the membership (see p. 88 below), the burdens of ultimate hierarchical accountability are considerably lightened. This organizational theory makes for good theological practice since, according to the tenets of religious freedom so forcefully outlined by Vatican II, ultimate accountability in matters religious must also be borne by individuals and communities before God. See "Declaration on Religious Freedom," art. 2 in W. Abbott, ed., *op. cit.*

21. See "Decree on the Ministry and Life of Priests," art. 6 in *ibid.*

22. The continuing education of the priest is an essential require-

ment for the due fulfillment of his cultic, prophetic and ministering offices in the modern church. Inasmuch as God ever speaks to his people in the present through new developments in theology and scientific progress, the priest's role is to relate the revealed Word of apostolic tradition to these new developments that God's truth may be coherently proclaimed in a contemporary context. Furthermore, as current research in liturgical studies and in the social and behavioral sciences suggests critical and constructive methods for implementing changes in worship, in mission and in pastoral care, the priest has the responsibility of utilizing these resources in celebrating a more communalizing liturgy with the people and in serving them with more personalizing ministry. Due to the technical nature of these studies and the need for competent presentation, it is quite apparent that these incessant role responsibilities of the priest can only be met by a full time professionally directed continuing education center. See "Pastoral Constitution on the Church in the Modern World," art. 62 and "Decree on the Ministry and Life of Priests," art. 19 in *ibid.*

23. The small local parishes of the latency models could readily be incorporated into this network; see above, pp. 73-75.

24. See G. Winter, *The Suburban Captivity of the Churches,* Doubleday, Garden City, N. Y., 1961, pp. 144-147. The author presents a similar plan for Protestant inner city ministry by sectionalizing areas of the metropolis into "cross-sectional" congregations according to major accessible transportation routes. His objective is to construct a scheme for an enduring bond between suburban parishes and the inner city as an ecclesial manifestation of "an interdependent community of the metropolis ministering to many different groups out of a common center" (p. 144).

25. For a brief but concise summary of some special skills needed in leading small groups, see Michael Argyle, *The Psychology of Interpersonal Behavior,* Penguin Books, Baltimore, 1967, pp. 96-101, 166-169. For some helpful empirical observations on the psycho-social dynamics of small group leadership and integration, see Robert F. Bales and Philip E. Slater, "Role Differentiation in Small Decision-Making Groups," in *Family, Socialization and Interaction Process,* by Talcott Parsons and Robert F. Bales, Free Press, Glencoe, Ill., 1955, pp. 259-306. This article also presents an interesting behavioral study on role differentiation in the small group which could be quite useful in determining a ministerial strategy for specific charismatic roles. The reader should also consult the last chapter of this book where Parsons and Bales employ the AGIL model to delineate the psycho-social "system problems" of the individual person, the nuclear family and the small group in the process of socialization and role differentiation. These are the precise problems which the priest would encounter in his role

of re-forming this level of society into Christian community (pp. 353-394).

26. The liturgical dimension of small group work in mission is not always accurately understood or appropriately valued. Its importance lies in the very purpose of the priest's mission to form an "aggregate" eucharistic community out of a small secular group in building up the body of Christ (Eph. 2:19-22). This social religious distinction is well-defined by Francois Houtart, *Sociology and Pastoral Care,* Franciscan Herald Press, Chicago, 1965, pp. 49-52.

27. It is, of course, correct to observe that the problems of latency and transition would exist in the integration models as critically as in the latency models. The choice of which model to utilize in implementing reform, however, would depend on the sociological conditions of the given area, the attitudes of the particular priest and people involved and the specific purposes of latency to preserve values or integration to preserve unity.

28. See Harvey Cox, *The Secular City,* Macmillan, N. Y., 1965, pp. 157-158.

29. See note 34 below.

30. For some important insights on how interdependent and specialized organizational roles are related to the administrative and political power of a hierarchical system, see Chandler Morse, "The Functional Imperatives," in *The Social Theories of Talcott Parsons,* ed. Max Black, Prentice-Hall, Englewood Cliffs, N. J., 1961, pp. 121, 151-152. In this essay, Morse proposes a slight variation of Parsonian theory for hierarchical systems to include a fifth functional imperative, namely, "superior coordination." This imperative could easily be applied to the hierarchical system of episcopal authority in the church and would be reflective of the bishop's supervisory role in the primitive church as administrative overseer (see R. Brown, *op. cit.,* pp. 37-38, 67-68). Such a biblical-organizational image of episcopal authority personalized in the role of a *superior coordinator* would indeed help to tie the bonds of its collegial expression and to decentralize the force of its political power.

31. On the importance of flexibility in authority relationships and its relation to innovation, see Wilbert E. Moore, *Social Change,* Prentice-Hall, Englewood Cliffs, N. Y., 1963, p. 13.

32. On the importance of institutionalizing change in societal structures, see Amitai Etzioni, *The Active Society,* Free Press, New York, 1968, pp. 14-15; and especially in church structures, see F. Houtart, *The Eleventh Hour, Explosion of a Church,* Sheed and Ward, New York, 1968, pp. 186-188.

33. Fichter, *op. cit.,* pp. 201-202; Schallert-Kelley, *op. cit.,* pp. 177-178.

34. The kind of dialogue needed to integrate the diversity of innovative pastoral forms in an ecumenical church is that exchange of openness in the pursuit of truth which inspires people to appreciate other forms and traditions. See Peter L. Berger, *A Rumor of Angels,* Doubleday, Garden City, N. Y., 1969, pp. 107-117; see also pp. 146-148 below.

Chapter IV

1. With the reactivation of the charismatic influence of the faithful in diversified ministries and participated liturgies, more cultic leaders will come forth from the people themselves, charismatically gifted to provide this direction. Heretofore, the ecclesiastical structures of the church and the canonical institution of the priesthood have all too often deemphasized the place of the Spirit in providing for cultic leaders. The institutionalization of ordination has marked the church with too many priests who do not know how to lead a liturgy. Obviously lacking the special charism for this purpose, they perform rites with such impersonal demeanor and perfunctorial gestures that their only title to a valid priesthood is through orders and jurisdiction. However necessary this title may be for the hierarchical traditions of the church, it must be recognized that cultic leaders are not made by imposing hands or canonical documents. Nor are they breeded by the impersonal ceremonies of irresponsive congregations. The special charism from the Spirit for leading worship is a fundamental prerequisite for any cultic leader and must be cultivated in the modern church by private prayer, by personal celebrations of responsive congregations and by professional training. As a matter of tradition, it should be remembered that in the early church, cultic leaders were known by their charismata (see J. Daniélou, *op. cit.,* pp. 349-350).

2. Again, the relationship between charism and office is of equal importance to the prophetic leader. What is particularly significant for a traditional and ecumenical understanding of this relationship is that the prophetic leader in some parts of the early church was also the cultic leader. See 1 Cor. 14:29-33; the *Didache,* X, 7; XIII, 3; and the *Shepherd* of Hermas, Mand. XI, 7-10.

3. See pp. 59-60 above and note 14 of chapter 3.

4. See "The United States of America vs. the Berrigans: Some Documents," "The Indictment" and "The Response of 'The Conspiracy'" in *The Berrigans,* eds. William VanEtten Casey and Philip Nobile, Avon Books, New York, 1971. pp. 220-237, 238-244, 245-247 respectively.

5. *Creative Ministry,* Doubleday, New York, 1971, p. 110.

6. See Pierre Teilhard de Chardin, *The Divine Milieu,* Harper Torchbooks, New York, 1965. In this religious classic, the author lays a theological foundation for the process of spiritual interaction in Christian ministry from pp. 140 to 146.

7. H. Nouwen, *op. cit.,* pp. 115-116.

8. For a clear discussion on the faithful's participation in the ministry of reconciliation and their relationship to the priest as leader, see J. Macquarrie, *op. cit.,* pp. 374-382 and 388.

9. See *The Jerusalem Bible,* note k.

10. *Discipleship and Priesthood,* Herder and Herder, New York, 1965, pp. 66-69.

11. See Teilhard de Chardin, *op. cit.,* pp. 102-104 and 115-117.

12. Notice how the formation of the faithful into a priestly people is described in this epistle in relation to their liturgical life, especially as regards baptism and the eucharist.

13. For a more detailed commentary on the liturgy of infant baptism and on its pastoral celebration as a means to form Christian community, see my article, "The New Rite of Infant Baptism," *Worship,* 43:4 (1969) 224-230.

14. K. Schelkle, *op. cit.,* pp. 74-75.

15. *Ibid.,* pp. 76-77.

16. Patristic imagery reflects this formative function of Christ's ministry of suffering service by picturing Jesus as forming the church from his sacred side as he slept on the cross. See St. Bonaventure, *The Tree of Life,* no. 30 in *The Works of Bonaventure, Mystical Opuscula I,* St. Anthony Guild Press, Paterson, N.J., 1960, p. 127.

17. See note m.

18. See *op. cit.,* pp. 101-104 and Robert L. Faricy, *Teilhard de Chardin's Theology of the Christian in the World,* Sheed and Ward, New York, 1967, pp. 168-172.

19. Theology Subcommittee of the National Conference of Catholic Bishops, *op. cit.,* quoted in *loc. cit.,* no. 4.

20. See J. Fichter, *op. cit.,* p. 206. See also E. Schein, *op. cit.,* pp. 35-37. Describing the style of contemporary professional work and its specialized roles, Schein illustrates the need for the professional school to prepare its students for the reality of specialization by engaging them in field-oriented team projects with ample opportunity for theoretical analysis through interdisciplinary research. He insists that, in addition to the acquisition of their own particular professional skills, students be equipped with other skills in applied behavioral science. He urges, furthermore, that the professional school take an active part in guiding the early career paths of its graduates to insure the proper application of their training and the continued growth of their learning. His approach to professional education is sorely needed in seminaries (see Fichter,

pp. 90-91) and could fittingly prepare priests with the necessary skills for their pivotal, relevant and peripheral roles of ministry in the service of the church and of society. (See note 16, chapter 3.)

21. In this regard, it is especially necessary to recognize a significant theological and organizational distinction involved in the selection of the priest's assignment. While a variety of choices for ministerial work should certainly be available to every priest and while the functions of the diocesan personnel board are precisely for the purpose of systematically providing this variety through professional managerial procedures, it must be remembered that the priest's choice not only depends on his personal interests and professional competency but ultimately rests upon the New Testament concept of election by God to serve his people (Heb. 5:1-10). This theological dimension to occupational selection thus gives primary importance to the needs of the diocese and to the roles of both the bishop and the particular community to be served in finalizing the appointment of the priest. On the rights of the local community in this matter, see H. Küng, *The Church*, p. 441.

22. See A. Greeley, "Principles of Personnel Policy," in *Secular Priest in the New Church*, ed. Gerard S. Sloyan, Herder and Herder, New York, 1967, pp. 166-175.

23. This right is founded on the charism of discernment (1 Cor. 12:10; 1 Jn. 4:1-3). See H. Kung, *The Church*, pp. 421-422 and 440.

24. *Pacem in Terris*, ed., William J. Gibbons, Paulist Press, Glen Rock, N. J., 1963, arts. 33-34, pp. 14-15.

Chapter V

1. See above, pp. 34-35.

2. R. McBrien, *op. cit.*, p. 172.

3. See *Democratization of the Church*, ed. Alois Muller (*Concilium*, vol. 63), Herder and Herder, New York, 1971, especially Norbert Greinacher, "A Community Free of Rule," pp. 87-107 and Raymund Kottje, "The Selection of Church Officials: Some Historical Facts and Experiences," pp. 117-126. See also note 21 of chapter 4 above.

4. See *A Greek-English Lexicon of the New Testament*, eds. William F. Arndt and F. Wilbur Gingrich, University of Chicago Press, Chicago, 1957, p. 436.

5. See Acts 26:18; Col. 1:12; 1 Peter 5:3; *The Epistles of Ignatius* to the Eph. 11:2, Rom. 1:2, Tral. 12:3, Phil. 5:1 and *The Martyrdom of Polycarp* 6:2. See also Gerhard Kittel, *Theological Dictionary of the New Testament*, Wm. B. Eerdmans Pub-

lishing Co., Grand Rapids, Michigan, 1965, vol. III, pp. 763-764.

6. See Robert Clyde Johnson, "The Christian Ministry," in *The Church and Its Changing Ministry,* ed. Robert Clyde Johnson, The General Assembly of the United Presbyterian Church in the United States of America, Philadelphia, 1961, p. 26.

7. In the eighteenth century, the word was used to describe one engaged in a learned or skilled profession. It was only later in the nineteenth century that the word came to be associated with one following an occupation as a means of livelihood. The prior usage is, of course, more consistent with an even earlier (fifteenth century) meaning, namely, one committed to a religious profession and with the original Latin meaning, from the root *"profiteri,"* one who has made a public profession of faith. See *The Oxford English Dictionary,* Oxford, 1933, vol. VIII, p. 1428.

8. See pp. 157-160 below.

9. *Op. cit.,* quoted in *loc. cit.,* no. 5.

10. Notice the congruity of describing the community of God's people in terms of a trust, as herein discussed, with the notion of the office of its hierarchical leader described in terms of a trusteeship, as discussed by Karl Lehmann. See "On the Dogmatic Justification for a Process of Democratization in the Church," in A, Muller, ed., *op. cit.,* pp. 81-83.

11. For a relevant explanation of this term see note 14 below.

12. See A. G. Martimort, "Preliminary Concepts" and "The Structure and Laws of Liturgical Celebration" in *The Church at Prayer, Introduction to the Liturgy,* ed. A. G. Martimort, Desclée Co., New York, 1968, pp. 12 and 58-60 respectively.

13. See Gabriel Moran, *A Design for Religion,* Herder and Herder, New York, 1971, pp. 97-102.

14. Notice that Moran defines education as "the improvement of human life through the devising of structures for learning" (*ibid.,* p. 146). The term "open education" is most significant for the purpose of drawing the ecclesiological role implications of Christian education. As this term deemphasizes that authoritarian structures of teaching that close in on the classroom, it redesigns education on communal structures for learning that open into the environment. Its application to the problems of religious education in the institutional church is well-advised by the words of Herbert Kohl: "The development of open, democratic modes of existence is essentially the problem of abandoning the authoritarian use of power and of providing workable alternatives. That is a problem that must be faced by all individuals and institutions that presume to teach" (*The Open Classroom,* The New York Review, New York, 1969, p. 16).

15. It is evident not only from this study but also from the

crisis of catechetics that more scientific research is critically needed in the areas of pastoral liturgy and religious education. See the *General Catechetical Directory* of the Sacred Congregation for the Clergy, United States Catholic Conference, Washington, 1971, pp. 94-95. As this document suggests, "questions that have not yet been researched" must be probed and this would include exploring new ways of reorienting children in and even to the church. The missiological role implications of church membership in the light of current ecclesiology impel us to re-examine the theology and to re-evaluate the liturgy of infant baptism. See my article, "Ecclesiology and Infant Baptism," *Worship*, 44:7 (1970) 433-437.

16. See G. Moran, *ibid.*, pp. 96-120 and Ronald Goldman, *Readiness for Religion*, Seabury Press, New York, 1970, pp. 77-199.

17. *Ibid.*, pp. 100-101.

18. "The Necessary Ecumenism," *Commonweal*, 91:5 (1969) 145-148.

19. *The Way of All the Earth*, Macmillan, New York, 1972, p. ix.

20. *Ibid.*, p. xi.

21. *Ibid.*, pp. 224-225.

22. *Ibid.*, pp. 220-221.

23. See Teilhard de Chardin, *How I Believe*, Harper and Row, New York, 1969, pp. 77-85.

24. *Ibid.*, p. 85.

25. This plan would be constructed from the Parsonian theories on the institutional factors of interorganizational integration. See T. Parsons, "Suggestions for a Sociological Approach to the Theory of Organizations," in *Administrative Science Quarterly*, I (June, 1956) pp. 63-85 and II (Sept. 1956) pp. 225-239; see also note 1 of chapter 3 above.